THE ELEMENTS OF THE CELTIC TRADITION

Caitlín Matthews is a writer, singer and harpist.
After her academic and drama school training, she went on to
discover and work in the Western Mystery Tradition. She has
contributed widely to the field of Celtic research, publishing
many important works on the subject and running very
popular workshops.

The *Elements Of* is a series designed to present high quality introductions to a broad range of essential subjects.

The books are commissioned specifically from experts in their fields. They provide readable and often unique views of the various topics covered, and are therefore of interest both to those who have some knowledge of the subject, as well as those who are approaching it for the first time.

Many of these concise yet comprehensive books have practical suggestions and exercises which allow personal experiences as well as theoretical understanding, and offer a valuable source of information on many important themes.

In the same series

Aborigine Tradition
Alchemy
The Arthurian Tradition
Astrology
Bahá'í Faith
Buddhism
Celtic Christianity
The Chakras
Christian Symbolism
Creation Myth
Dreamwork
The Druid Tradition
Earth Mysteries
Feng Shui
The Goddess
The Grail Tradition
The Greek Tradition

Herbalism
Human Potential
Islam
Meditation
Mysticism
Native American Traditions
Natural Magic
Pendulum Dowsing
Prophecy
Psychosynthesis
Qabalah
Shamanism
Sufism
Tai Chi
Taoism
Visualisation
Zen

THE ELEMENTS OF

THE CELTIC TRADITION

Caitlín Matthews

ELEMENT

Shaftesbury, Dorset ● Rockport, Massachusetts
Brisbane, Queensland

First published in Great Britain in 1989 by
Element Books Limited
Longmead, Shaftesbury, Dorset

Published in the USA in 1991 by
Element, Inc.
42 Broadway, Rockport, MA 01966

Published in Australia by
Element Books Limited for
Jacaranda Wiley Limited
33 Park Road, Milton, Brisbane 4064

Reprinted September 1989, December 1989,
August 1991, November 1991,
August 1992, November 1992,
February 1993

Designed by Jenny Liddle
Cover illustration by David James
Cover design by Max Fairbrother
Printed and bound in Great Britain by
Biddles Ltd, Guildford & King's Lynn

British Library Cataloguing in Publication Data
Matthews, Caitlín 1952 –
The elements of the Celtic tradition.
1. Celtic myths
I. Title
293′.13

Library of Congress Cataloging in Publication
Data available

ISBN 1-85230-075-2

CONTENTS

A Dhiarmuid

Beannocht leó a los a saoire,
dronga ar nár cheisd cruadhlaoighe,
am coimhthionál dar chóir searc,
doircheadhán dóibh nir dhoircheacht.

Blessings upon their noble nature,
to whom complex poems were no hardship;
to that beloved gathering of poets
the darkest verse was daylight dawning.

[Our mother is memory.]

ACKNOWLEDGEMENTS

Prime among the acknowledgements for this book must stand the great company of poets, storytellers and scholars, known and unknown, who have been true bearers of tradition. It is by their light and upon the paths that they have trodden, that I have made this interior pilgrimage. To them, praise and honour! I hope that this bare recital of their wisdom may lead others to hear the silver branch and find their way to the great Tree of Tradition. Thanks are due:

To my husband, John, thanks for gathering together most of the literary sources for this book. As the *llyfrgellydd* of our *teulu*, he must by now have worked off several lifetimes of sacerdotal librarianship.

To my son, Emrys, as ever: many thanks for letting your mother play with her computer when you had more exciting games to share.

To my soul-friend, Diarmuid, for expert guidance far beyond the ninth wave of known textual sources. He is the real pilot of this book.

To the Company of Hawkwood, especially those who convened the grove of the Mysteries of Taliesin in December 1988, and to all fellow-students of the Celtic realms who have guided and advised by their personal experience of the enduring tradition.

To the Order of Bards, Ovates and Druids, and all who meet in the inner groves.

To Christian-J. Guyonvarc'h and Françoise Le Roux for their painstaking research and translations of rare Celtic textual sources.

To Kaledon Naddair for providing me with a copy of Monard's *A Druidic Calendar*.[80]

To Simon Franklin for suggesting this book: thank you for your enthusiastic support.

INTRODUCTION:
THE CELTIC REALMS

My brief in this little book has been to give the reader an introduction to the mysterious inner world of the Celts and to examine the empowerments of their myth and magic. It is not intended to be a history of the Celtic races nor a compendious mythology detailing each god and goddess.

I have chosen to deal primarily with the British and Irish Celtic traditions, rather than with those of the Continental Celts. The reasons for this are easily explained. The insular Celts of the British Isles, particularly of Ireland, were relatively undisturbed by other cultures longer than the Celts of the Continent. They thus retained their traditions longer than their Continental relatives. These were subsequently transmitted from oral to literary tradition during the so-called Dark Ages through to the late Middle Ages. It is to these sources that I have gone for my researches rather than to commentaries or ill-informed guesswork.

We should bear in mind that the Celts did not call themselves this, nor did they speak 'Celtic'. They thought of themselves as Bretons. Irish, British or Gaels. Earlier than the Roman invasion, they probably thought of themselves as 'the people of such-and-such tribe'. The use of the word 'Celtic' in this book is merely convenient. We should also remember that the Celts are a family of people continually moving throught time and adapting to new parameters. The migratory Celts of the Hallstat culture in the fourth century BC were not identical in behaviour and custom to those living in Gaelic Scotland in the fourth century AD.

I have attempted to uncover the essential core of what made the Celts Celtic by going directly to the source texts, though some consider these to be suspect, since the texts were written down from oral transmission in the early to late Middle Ages and often bear a decidedly Christian tinge. (In one story, for example, druids worship a golden calf in a manner more reminiscent of Aaron than of real Celts.) However, we must admit that these were frequently transcribed from oral tradition exactly as they were memorised, with great faithfulness, for that was how the old stories, genealogies and poems had to be preserved.

In our examination of the myth and magic preserved in the old texts we must proceed with both caution and confidence. These stories do not portray soap-opera characters living out kitchen-sink dramas: kings are noble, women beautiful, warriors brave, druids cunning and resourceful, poets lyrical. We are in the land of mythic archetype where the stories unfold in a symbolic and culturally consistent manner. The action always keeps one foot in the Other-world and the frequent appearance of gods as animals or super-humans is not unusual. So while we should be wary of applying contemporary psychological values to the characters we will meet in these pages, we may with confidence listen to what they are telling us about the Celtic world.

Since so many books on Celtic material tend to rehash the same material, I have striven to go out of the way for different and often more illuminating texts. Currently, only about 25 per cent of Celtic texts are translated into English and of these, few are readily available to the reader. On page 122 there is a full bibliography of the books and articles consulted for this work. If you wish to study more deeply, try to read some of these, especially the original texts in translation: they will give you a firsthand flavour of the Celtic realms which no one's commentary can convey. This book cannot begin to tell the vast range of stories and myths which underpin its pages. Read all you can lay hands on whether source text or retelling, Celtic epic poetry or folk-story.

I have avoided mention of the Arthurian legends and the Grail tradition, since these are amply dealt with in two other books in this series, but the reader will find illuminating cross-references to the Celtic world in both these traditions.[75,76]

Those new to the Celtic Realms will find a great wealth of wisdom which can only be hinted at in these pages. Those who are already experienced travellers in these lands may be inspired to learn a Celtic language.

For those who wish to make the Celtic Realms their own spiritual *modus operandi*, I have included a few practical exercises derived from the traditional material of this book. (See p. 115)

Whatever your persuasion, I hope that this condensed study will make you a soul-friend of the Celtic tradition, and that you will continue to derive great nourishment from the world of myth and magic.

The superior numbers in the text refer to the numerated bibliography on p. 122.

Caitlín Matthews
11 January 1989

1·THE HOLY GROUND

Where did the Celts come from? Even scholars cannot agree. Myles Dillon and Nora Chadwick dated the first Celtic settlements in the British Isles to the early Bronze Age (about 1180 BC), and have even identified the Beaker Folk as proto-Celts.[8] Leon E. Stover and Bruce Kraig, inferring certain evidence from prehistoric Wessex and Hungary, have suggested that the Celts have an even earlier origin, around about the third millennium BC.[99] The claims of nineteenth-century linguists and ethnographers for an Indo-European origin for the Celts have been largely overset, though, linguistically and culturally, we can still find considerable evidence to support this.[96]

Whatever the truth of the matter, origins are hard to establish with any certainty. Since even scholarly opinion cannot find consensus in this matter and as this is a book dealing primarily with the myth and magic of the Celts, it is perhaps more fitting that we stick to mythic origins, since these are inevitably what people remember most clearly.

The Celts are known to have established themselves in Europe, in a wide swathe from what is now Hungary to the Western seaboard of Europe, during.the first millennium BC. Their distinctive art and tribal customs are known to us through archaeology and through the observations of Classical writers. In the fourth-century BC, the Greek writer Ephoros said that the Celts were one of four great barbarian people of the (known) world: the Libyans in Africa, the Persians in

1

Portal dolmen

the East and, in Europe, the Scythians and the Celts.[44]

It is interesting to see which mythic origins have been consciously adopted. The Irish traced their roots back to Scythia, Egypt, Spain and Lochlan (Scandinavia), and, after the adoption of Christianity, the Family of Noah. The British trace their origins back to Troy, preferring to keep the Classical line of transmission open. It is difficult to say with what accuracy the British or Irish conceived their ancestry before the times of either the Four Masters or Geoffrey of Monmouth, both of whom 'preserved' these traditions and thus enshrined them for all time afterwards.

INVASIONS FROM BEYOND THE NINTH WAVE

'Some peoples, such as the Romans, think of their myths historically, the Irish think of their history mythologically'.[98] This statement stands for all Celtic peoples, but it is among the Irish texts that we find the most compelling evidence for conscious mythic history. The *Book of Invasions* details the waves of invaders who came to Ireland, and is an attempt to synthesise bardic and oral memory with biblical tradition. The result is a magical epic of intricate detail, giving a wealth of story.[15]

In Celtic tradition, the ninth wave was the designated boundary of the land, beyond which were the neutral seas and foreign countries. To be exiled was to 'go beyond the ninth wave'. Frequently we read of this most extreme of Celtic punishments for offenders: to be set adrift in a boat with neither oars, sails nor rudder, with only a knife and some fresh water. At the mercy of the seas, few survived, but those who did were fated to perform great deeds which shape the outcome of history.

Six races arrive in Ireland from beyond the ninth wave: the company of Cessair, the granddaughter of Noah; the company of Partholon; the people of Nemed; the Fir Bolg or Men of the Bag; the Tuatha de Danaan or the Children of Danu; and the Milesians. Of these, the Fir Bolg become the aboriginal baddies of Irish tradition, while the Tuatha de Danaan are remembered as the godlike race. With the coming of the Milesians, they take up residence in the hollow hills of the *sidhe*, later dwindling in status to the Good Folk, the Faeries.

It is perhaps the Tuatha de Danaan who are best known and remembered, for they have heroic and godlike stature in the many stories related about them. They are said to have had three classes of people among them:

tuathach — Chiefs
dé — Gods
dàn — Craftsmen and gifted people

But despite their splendid exploits, they are overcome by the Milesians, the race of the Gaels, from whom are partially descended the inhabitants of modern Ireland and Western Scotland.

The British parallel to the *Book of Invasions* is Geoffrey of Monmouth's *History of the Kings of Britain*,[9] which opts for the Classical antecedents of the British. Geoffrey's book continues the story begun in the *Iliad* and the *Aeneid*, giving the Britons Trojan forebears. Taliesin, Britain's greatest Celtic poet, speaks of himself as a prophet 'to the remnant of Troy'. Embedded in British tradition are scant references to the history of earlier races. In the *Mabinogion* and early Welsh genealogies, it is clear that the Roman invasion passed into folk memory as both a grievous and momentous event which overlaid most earlier invasions.[17]

There is a fragmentary story concerning the contention of the British king Caswallawn (Cassivelaunus) and Julius Caesar over the love of Fflur, who may be a representative of Britain's own Goddess of Sovereignty.[72] It is also clear that Geoffrey of Monmouth's work owes much to an earlier, lost history. But the assimilation of Rome subsequently became the cause of British nostalgia during the Middle Ages. Wales, struggling under the Norman yoke, eulogised its past glories under Rome and rejoiced in kings descended from Roman generals and governors.

Within British memory was the story of how Brittany was colonised. The men who fought with Macsen Wledig (the historical Magnus Maximus) desired land of their own and so they went into Armorica and killed its men, married its women and cut out their tongues, lest the pure British speech be corrupted.[17] This mythic tale has part of its basis in fact, for we know that Britons had settled in Armorica during the confusion of the Roman withdrawal from Britain. Magnus Maximus's troops did leave Britain partially undefended and might well have settled in Brittany.

Similar stories to the one about cutting out the women's tongues are encountered in folk tradition, especially in regard to earlier races. The godlike family of Llyr betray traces of foreign origin. since their father is called Llyr Llediath or Half-tongue; Bran, his eldest son, is of titanic stature, unlike the race of Britain.[31]

And so it is that races tell mythic stories about their origins, enhancing their lineage by relationship with gods and heroes, and creating subtle alignments with the Otherworld from which emanate all beginnings and continuances.

THE SHADOW OF ATLANTIS

Inundations or floods play their part in the mythical history of the Celts. One of the major myths of Western Europe is the Fall of Atlantis – the great land whose esoteric and technological brilliance was of little use against the elements. Wild theories have raged about the great civilisations of the ancient world having stemmed from Atlantean culture, but we find little concerning the legacy of the Celts in this regard.

The submerging of Ys remains one of the greatest Breton stories. It tells how Gradlon, King of Ys, had a daughter who worked the old magic. She was Dahut, who took from her father's neck the key of the dyke which protected the city of Ys from the sea. St Guenolé warned Gradlon of impending disaster and he mounted his horse to flee the engulfing waves which Dahut had let loose. Dahut and Ys were drowned utterly.[56]

Britain has its own fragmentary tradition concerning the inundation of Cantre'r Gwaelod, in Cardigan Bay.

In *The Black Book of Caermarthen*, we read a variant in which a maiden called Mererid uncovers 'the fountain of Venus' after having been raped by Seithennin. These two stories, combined with certain other references in the early Grail stories[72] reveal a female guardian of a source, well or spring which should not be uncovered, but due to some primal violation, the waters are revealed and overwhelm the land. This Maiden of the Waters is so anciently embedded in Celtic tradition that she has no name, merely a title. Her presence is traceable in the myths of Boann, Ceridwen, Liban and Cessair.

And so while it is the biblical deluge which is documented in the *Lebor Gabála Erenn*, it is perhaps to some vague memory of Atlantis and the spring-guarding maiden that some of the stories look in their primeval vision.

THE NAMING OF THE LAND

The name of the land has always been of great importance to its people since it bears all the mythic weight of tradition with it. Not surprising, as peoples have come and gone, so have the names changed. *The White Book of Rhydderch* gives the names of Britain as follows:

> The first name that this Island bore, before it was taken or settled: Myrddin's Precinct. And after it was taken and settled, the Island of Honey. And after it was conquered by Prydein, son of Aedd the Great, it was called the Island of Prydein (Britain).[31]

Keating's *History of Ireland* gives a similar, though longer, list for the former names of Ireland. Some are descriptive and others eponymous:

1. The Island of the Woods: because 'Ireland was one continuous wood'.
2. Country of Remote Limits
3. The Noble Island; called so during the time of the Fir Bolg
4. Eire ⎫
5. Fódla ⎬ all named after Goddesses
6. Banba ⎭
7. Inis Fail: called the Island of Fail from the Lia Fail or Stone of Destiny
8. The Island of Pigs: called so by the Milesians, who only saw a misty island in the shape of a pig when they tried to land there,

for it had been enchanted by the Tuatha de Danaan.
9. Scotia: after the mother of the Milesians[62]

This variety of names hides the fact that, for the Celts, the land itself was mystically at one with the Goddess of the Land. She has many names and is sought by many suitors:

> The mighty lady Eriu,
> Erimón harried her,
> Ir, Eber sought for her –
> I seek the land of Ireland.[15]

When the Milesians seek to invade Ireland, they encounter three aspects of the Goddess of the Land: Banba, Fodla and Eriu. Their spokesman, Amergin the poet, in an episode reminiscent of the Judgement of Paris, promises each goddess that her name shall become that of the island. At Tara, the Milesians are exiled from the land and Amergin judges that the fleet shall sail beyond the ninth wave and then return. They engage in magical battle with the Tuatha de Danaan and Amergin sings a great mystical poem which enables his people to take Ireland for their own.

DINDSENCHAS

The *dindsenchas*, or place-name stories, represent the historical topography of Ireland. They preserve the native 'song-lines', the mythic stories which connect the gods to the land. In British tradition, there is Nennius, who preserves the Seven Wonders of Britain in much the same way, though in far more abbreviated form.[22] It was left to Gerald of Wales to record the remnants of myth and folklore associated with Wales.[12]

The importance of these texts cannot be measured since, although some of the stories are onomastic (being worked up to explain a given name), some do preserve authentic traditions about the site which is sained by use, custom and the story about its guardian spirit.

We come near the roots of the Celtic understanding of the Gods and their association with the land in this extract from the *Rennes Dindsenchas*:

One day Catháir had a vision of a beautiful woman. She was the daughter of 'a hundreded hospitaller' and she was clothed in rainbow raiment and was pregnant. 'Eight hundred years she

6

was thus, until she brought forth a manchild, and on the day he was born he was stronger than his mother. They began to fight, and his mother found no place to avoid him save by going through the midst of the son. A lovely hill was over the heads of them both; higher than every hill with hosts thereon. A shining tree like gold stood on the hill; because of its height it would reach to the clouds. In its leaves was every melody; and its fruits, when the wind touched it, specked the ground.'

Unable to understand this vision, Catháir sent for his druid, Brí, to interpret for him. 'The damsel [is] the river which hath the name of Slaney. These are the colours of her raiment, artists of every kind without sameness of distinction or peculiarity. This is the hundreded hospitaller who was her father, the Earth through the which come a hundred of every kind. This is the son who was in her womb for eight hundred years, the lake which will be born of the stream of the Slaney, and in time it will come forth. Many hosts there, every one a-drinking from the river and the lake. This is the great hill above their heads, the power over all. This is the tree with the colour of gold and with its fruits, though over Banba (Ireland) in its sovranty. This is the music that was in the tops of the tree, the eloquence in guarding and correcting the judgements of the Gaels. This is the wind that would tumble the fruit, thy liberality in dispensing jewels and treasures.'[24]

In this extract, Catháir himself partakes of the earth's goodness and the vision is properly a prophecy of his reign. The natural contours and features of the land appear in his dream with the semblance of men and women, which is exactly how humankind has visualised its first deities.

In the riddling wooing of Emer by Cuchulainn, the hero is asked which way he travelled. He replies, not giving the generally accepted names of places, but 'in the secret language of poets', giving instead the glosses from the *Dindsenchas*:

From the Cover of the Sea, over the Great Secret of the Tuatha de Danaan, and the Foam of the two steeds of Emain Macha; over the Morrigu's Garden, and the Great Sow's Back; over the Glen of the Great Dam, between god and his prophet; over the Marrow of the Woman Fedelm, between the boar and his dam; over the Washing-place of the horses of Dea; between the King of Ana and his servant, to Monnchuile of the Four Corners of the World; over Great Crime and the Remnants of the Great Feast; between the Vat and the Little Vat, to the gardens of Lug, to the daughters of Tethra's nephew, Forgall, the king of the Fomorians.[6]

To anyone knowing the place-name stories of Ireland, none of these kennings would be obscure, and so it is that Emer is able to trace Cuchulainn's itinerary exactly.

CREATION AND COSMOLOGY

For the Celts, there are no myths of creation as such. The ongoing chain of existences – of land, tree, bird, animal, humanity, heroes, beings and gods – is a continuum which is recreated from within a shifting cosmology. Thus we will examine the stories of origination last in this book, in true Celtic fashion. (See Chapter 10.)

The Celts conceived themselves to be potentially existent in all worlds, in the sense that they related to each part of their cosmology in different, intimate ways. It was considered easy to pass between the worlds of the created realms and the Otherworld. This proximity occasioned specific rituals of propitiation in which the very young were guarded from accidentally straying into the Otherworld. Heroes might venture between the worlds, fortified by courage alone; poets and druids might travel thence, secure in wisdom and knowledge; but the sick and the young were vulnerable and might not return. It was so that the sick were watched over continually and children were given childhood names, which hid their potential virtues.

The Otherworld in Celtic myth is an inscape of or overlay upon the land. It has its specified gateways or crossing-places but it is not conceived of as being 'up or out there'. Rather it is contiguous with every part of life. (See Chapter 6.)

In the poem, *Preiddeu Annwn*, the underworld is reached by sea, just as the Irish *immrama* (wonder-voyages) take ship to the Blessed Islands. However, the British underworld of Annwn is also reached by entry into the earth, through springs and by travelling overland to another valley, as well as by crossing a river and chasing a (usually white) beast, as many characters within the *Mabinogion* attest.[72]

In the poems of Taliesin, we find the Christianised, distanced stance of Classical cosmology, but the old Celtic Otherworld is also present with all its intensity of image, colour and symbol.[78] Taliesin appears in the *Vita Merlini* as Telgesinus. He visits Merlin ostensibly to teach him about the nature of winds and rain-storms. In the course of this passage he describes the creation out of the four elements, the establishment of five earthly zones and a three-part heaven: the starry heaven, inhabited by angels; the airy heaven, under the stars, but above the moon, thronged with mediating daemons; and the sublunary realm, inhabited by illusory demons. Then he describes seas, the kinds of fish in the seas inhabiting them; he further enumerates the major islands of the Northern Hemisphere, including Insula Pomorum or the Island of Apples – Britain's Avalon. Springs are described and their health-giving benefits, birds and their habits.[10]

While much of this natural history and geography are taken from the monk, Isidore of Seville (560–636) – a not impossible historical contemporary of Taliesin's – it is doubtless that Taliesin is here shown exercising a very druidic function in teaching the basic components of inner and outer cosmology. A similar list is given in the Irish *Senchas Mor*, an exhaustive compilation of legal precedents, giving the divisions of time, the winds, the planets and earthly zones.[27]

THE COSMIC GAMING BOARD

For the Celts, cosmology was measured by mythology and festival. Their myths reveal an ordered pattern upon which random actions can happen. It is not without significance that the gaming board, the British *gwyddbwyll* or the Irish *fidhchell* board should figure largely in many stories, for it is upon the regular squares of Celtic cosmology that the gods and heroes move.

There is one world, one king, one year, one cosmic shape, in which

Table 1:1 The Four Mystical Directions

Direction	Region	Otherworldly city	Gift	Master	Evangelist
North	Ulster	Falias	Stone	Morfessa	John
East	Leinster	Gorias	Spear	Esras	Luke
South	Munster	Finias	Sword	Uscias	Mark
West	Connacht	Murias	Cauldron	Semias	Matthew

things happen. And yet, things are not that simple, for the Celtic world is shot with the uncertainty and random influence of the

Otherworld, whose gateways lie ever open to surprise and entrap the unwary.

In Ireland there is a fourfold shape to this board which is governed by four directions, four mystical regions, four masters of tradition, to whom we can add their later Christian analogues. (See Table 1.1.) The four Otherworldly cities given in Table 1:1 are the places whence the Tuatha de Danaan derive. The gifts were given them by the masters of those cities, and constitute their sovereign power in Ireland. (See Chapter 3.)

On the gaming board, which is also the land, there is always a sacred centre – which is seldom geographically central! The mystical fifth dimension or centre of this symbolic pattern is the Otherworld itself, typified in Irish tradition by Tara, the seat of the High Kings. But each country has its own centres which, over the ages shift and change according to tribal boundaries.[95]

In the story of 'Lludd and Llefelys', the country is terrorised every May-Eve by a spectral screaming which causes barrenness in fields, women and animals and which causes the old and the young to die and the strong to lose their strength. Lludd discovers that this is caused by the national dragon and a foreign dragon contending on this night. He is advised to dig a hole at the very centre of his kingdom (designated as Oxford) and there he entraps both of them in a stone chest which he then orders to be buried at Dinas Emrys in North Wales. This story presents an interesting glimpse into the nature of sacred centres, for the dragons are captured at the seat of learning and are held in the mountain stronghold of Snowdonia.[17,72]

The interrelation of these sacred centres and the festivals which marked the Celtic year are discussed further in Chapter 8.

THE TABLE OF THE AIRTS

The airts, or the directions of the compass (see Fig. 1:1) have their own lore in Celtic tradition: not unusual in a people living on the Western seaboard of Europe to whom the sea, its tides, currents and winds, were of such importance. Each of the directions has its own wind, each having a distinctive colour.[27]

It is interesting to listen to modern fishermen on any part of the Celtic seaboard describing the weather: they frequently speak of a black wind and preserve their own lore about the table of the airts.

The Celts favoured deosil, or sunwise, as a direction – a fact which appears in many texts. It was contrary for many heroes to go

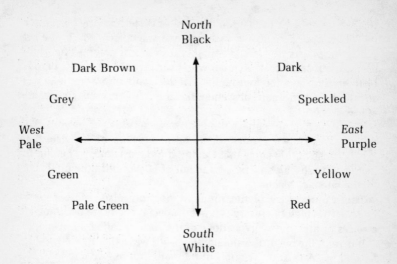

North
Black

Dark Brown   Dark

Grey   Speckled

West   East
Pale   Purple

Green   Yellow

Pale Green   Red

South
White

Fig. 1:1 The Table of the Airts

widdershins at all, and many kings were prohibited from making a circuit of their land in any way but deosil. This lore of the sacred direction is still preserved in modern Irish Catholic pilgrimages. Many sacred sites, holy to the memory of a Celtic saint – and often also to a Celtic god – have certain stations or mounds of stones, about which pilgrims circulate, always turning deosil, while reciting prayers.

Triplicities and the Ninefold

Sacred to Celtic numerology was the number three and its compound number, nine. One of the common features of the Celtic world is the importance given to triplicities. Goddesses come in clumps of three. The Welsh Triads preserve traditions by means of terse, mnemonic triplicities of information, from which a bard could relate several complex tales:

> Three Bestowed Horses of the Island of Britain:
> Meinlas, the mount of Caswallawn son of Beli,
> Melyngan Mangre, the mount of LLeu Llaw Gyffes,
> and Lluagor, the mount of Caradawg Strong-Arm.[31]

Typical of this concept of triplicities is the ninefold curse which

11

the goddess Macha calls upon the men of Ulster. Having been forced by Ulster's king to run a race against his horses while she was pregnant, Macha delivers her twin children untimely: 'At her delivery, she screamed that any man who heard would suffer the pains of birth for five days and four nights. All the Ulaid who were there were so afflicted and their descendants suffered for nine generations afterwards.'[98]

This is a powerful curse – nine half days for nine generations. This debility was known as the noinend or the 'novena' of the Ulstermen. It is because of this curse that Cuchulainn later comes to defend the passes to Ulster alone, since he is not of Ulster and thus unaffected by the curse of Macha.

This Celtic sense of the ninefold possibly also influenced the manner in which the rosary is prayed: special needs are petitioned in a series of nine daily invocations of the rosary, called a novena.

It is from the magical waters of the ninth wave that Blodeuwedd is formed by Math and Gwydion in their attempt to find a wife who is not of mortal race for the unfortunate Lleu Llaw Gyffes.[17]

The British Otherworldly fortress of Caer Nefenhir (Castle of the Highest Heaven), which appears in both 'Culhwch and Olwen' and 'Cad Goddeu',[78] is said to have nine natures.

Celtic tradition speaks frequently of a ninefold sisterhood. The sisters are said to guard and tend the cauldron of rebirth in the depths of Annwn, cooling it with their breath. In his description of Insula Pomorum, Taliesin speaks of them by name:

> That is the place where nine sisters exercise a kindly rule over those who come to them from our land. The one who is first among them has greater skill in healing, as her beauty surpasses that of her sisters. Her name is Morgen, and she has learned the uses of all plants in curing the ills of the body. She knows, too, the art of changing her shape, of flying through the air, like Daedelus, on strange wings. . . . They say she had taught astrology to her sisters – Moronoe, Mazoe, Gliten, Glitonea, Gliton, Tyronoe and Thiten – famous for her lyre.[10]

These eight women, with Morgen, make nine sisters. Morgen, the earliest appearance of Morgan le Fay of Arthurian tradition, is shown here in her obvious Celtic guise as healer and shapeshifter.[72]

THE PLEDGE OF THE ELEMENTS

The nature of the Celtic temperament is best summed up by the famous Gaulish oath: 'If I break faith with you, may the skies fall upon me, may the seas drown me, may the earth rise up and swallow me.' For the Celts, life was a passionate affair, an all or nothing enterprise. This great oath calls the very elements to witness; it also attests to the understanding that the land and the gods are one. This holistic concept of deity is a primal one with which we are out of tune today, secure in the belief that we have 'conquered' the elements.

The Celts had no such illusions. For them, the elements were the most powerful manifestations of the gods, not to be trifled with. It is so that this great oath is the most solomn pledge to the elements to destroy whoever does not keep faith.

Merlin in his madness in the Caledon Forest himself refers to the Elemental Pledge:

Since the battle of Arfderydd I have been unmoved by everything,
Even though the sky were to fall or the sea to overflow.

(my trans.)

The great powers so invoked may be personified by Lugh, the Morrighan and Banba in Irish tradition; by Lleu, Manawyddan and Rhiannon in British tradition, although there are numerous other deities who would serve as well as representatives of these elemental powers. It is to these that we turn next, for it is only within the great figures of the gods that we begin to understand the Celtic genius and its enduring strength.

2•THE PRIMAL GODS

THE SECRET GODS

When the Gaulish commander Brennus attacked Delphi and plundered it of its gold, he was said to have laughed aloud at seeing the temple there, at the way in which the Greeks depicted their gods in human representational form.[71] No doubt, to his Celtic mind, this custom seemed childishly immature, if not barbarously irreverent, for the gods could not be bounded by wood, metal or stone. How was it possible for a god, who could shapeshift into myriads of forms, animal, human and divine, to appear in only one shape? We tend to overlook the fact that the majority of statues depicting Celtic deities occur after exposure to Classical culture. Representational images before that time are usually symbolic, suggestive rather than completely depicted, so that the many aspects of the god are not frozen into a finite image. Aspectual deity is something almost forgotten in the West. The Christian Trinity is all that remains in our society. That we once possessed this facility for comprehending one deity under many forms is evident when we look at Celtic mythology. In common with the Indian gods, with whom they share a common root, the Celtic deities are multi-form, often ambivalent and pervasive of each other's territories and forms.

Just how the Celts conceived of their gods is very difficult to know, since, in every recorded story, people refuse to name their deity, always saying, 'I swear by the gods that my people swear by . . .' This secrecy warded the gods from the scrutiny of outsiders, for only tribal members might partake in the mystery of their god, which

14

Triple Mothers

included the knowing of his or her names and titles. And so, our knowledge of Celtic mythology is a tentative mixture of speculative archaeology and texts transcribed during the early Middle Ages.

There is no doubt that the Celts, wherever they originated, fused with the native peoples of Britain and Ireland, incorporating their beliefs and customs into their own culture. The *Dindsenchas* provide an interesting parable demonstrating this. The story concerns the naming of the hill of Uisnech in Meath. According to legend, Midhe, a druid of the Milesians, one of the last people to invade Ireland, lit a fire on that hill, where it burned for seven years. From this fire were lit all the fires of Ireland. But the native druids of Eire considered this an insult and they met together in council to debate the matter. Midhe had all their tongues cut out and buried in the earth of Uisnech, upon which he then sat. His mother then said: 'It is *Uaisnech* [proudly] you sit up there this night.' Which gave Uisnech its name.[88]

This incident, like many recorded in the *Dindsenchas*, is not a historical event but a teaching story. To cut out the tongues of the native priesthood is the act of a conqueror who wishes to create his own rules and abolish those of the native tradition. It is also a symbolic way of implying that the chief hill of assembly becomes sained with the lore of those mutilated druids, thus becoming a place of judgement and a prime, wisdom-giving mound.

The Celtic gods are primarily associated with the land in whose hills, rivers, valleys, caves, inlets and mountains they can still be found.

15

THE GREAT MOTHER AND HER TRIBE

It is impossible to deal with Celtic mythology in the same way that we approach Classical mythology, since it defies the pigeonhole categories beloved of scholars. Solar and lunar gods, deities who are patrons of particular skills, extended pantheons of interrelated gods and goddesses do not figure largely among the Celts. Goddesses do not appear as consorts, in subservient mode: rather, certain kings and heroes are consorts of goddesses.

In this chapter, I have chosen to present the unique categories of Celtic deity rather than attempt an impossible round-up of the entire corpus. The nature of the gods will become apparent in succeeding chapters, through their acts and interrelationship with kings, druids and heroes.

All texts are unanimous in according the first place to the tribal mother of the Celtic peoples: Anu, Danu or Don. Since the Celts were known to have settled from as far east as Czechoslovakia westwards, it is tempting to consider the etymology of this name as common to that from which the rivers Don, Dneiper, Dniester and Danube, the great rivers which flow across Europe, derive.

The Great Mother of the Gods is less clearly focused than other deities, because she stands at the head of the tribe, back before oral tradition can remember. As Danu, she is called 'the Mother of the Irish Gods',[25] though of course, as Don, she figures as the ancestress of the British ones also. *Cormac's Glossary* associates her with Brigit and mentions that 'The Paps of Anu', a distinctive hill-feature in Kerry, are named for the Great Mother.

Just as there are correlations between Greek and Roman myth, so too are there correspondences between the Irish family of Danu and the British family of Don: the gods Lugh and Lleu, Goibhniu and Gofannon, Manannan and Manawyddan are almost exact correlatives of each other, although their individual myths show greater variance.

Less obvious are the Irish/British correlations of Nuadu of the Silver Arm with Lludd Llaw Ereint (both gods have a silver hand or arm made for them) or Blanaid with Blodeuwedd (both women come from the Otherworld and betray their husbands); although it is evident from close examination of their stories that each pair shares a common origin.

Celtic tradition has no goddess of love, though it has many goddesses of wisdom. Prime among these is Brigit, the daughter of the Dagda. She inherited many of the qualities of Danu, becoming a

special patron to poets, smiths and healers. Like many other goddesses, she appears under three aspects. Brigit has perhaps had the
longest enduring cult of any Celtic goddess, since aspects of her were
subsumed into the cult of St Brigit of Kildare.

As the progenetrix of the tribe, Danu, or Don, ritually mates with
her chosen partner:

> The union of the god of the tribe with the goddess of the earth,
> of Sucellos with Nantosuelta, of the Dagda with the Morrighan,
> or with Boann, projects on the place of mythology what the
> union of the king with the animal incarnation of the goddess
> realizes on the plane of ritual, namely the marriage of the
> human group with the fertile soil, which is the necessary
> condition for the prosperity of the tribe and the purpose of all
> religious activity.'[98]

The bounty of the Great Goddess is shown in many different ways.
The capacious bag which Rhiannon gives to Pwyll, and Ceridwen's
skin bag, in which Taliesin is cast into the sea, are also aligned to this
theme. In British tradition, the Great Mother is given her own
constellation, Llys Don, the Court of Don or Cassiopaeia. From this
starry throne, she still rules her numerous tribe.

We will examine many other aspects of the Goddess in later
chapters.

The Good God

The Dagda of the Tuatha de Danaan has two other names which
perhaps help us to place his archetype: Eochaid Ollathair, or Father
of All, and Ruadh Rofessa, or 'The Red One of Perfect Knowledge'.
He is the old, cunning one whose crudity masks a wealth of
knowledge.

He is described as the King of the Tuatha de Danaan, and his name,
Dagda, or Good God, is explained so: 'for it was he performed
miracles and saw to the weather and the harvest.'[8] His stature arises
partially from his assertion at the council preceding the Battle of Mag
Tuiread at which all the gods each declare what they shall perform
for the common good. The Dagda says: 'All that you promise to do I
shall do myself alone.' Thus he shows himself to be a god who is
good at everything.[98] This feature is shared with Lugh, who is given
the name *Samildanach* or 'The Many-Gifted One'.

This inclusiveness of skills derives from the fact that the Dagda is
described as the god of *draídecht* or druidry, 'for it is he that had the

perfection of heathen science, and it is he that had the multiform triads'.[88] This formidable set of accomplishments make him a *samildanach* among druids.

The Dagda is famous for his great feats. When his son Oengus goes to ask for the hand of Etain Echrade, he is told he can only have her if the twelve lands of her father Ailill are cleared of forests to make an assembly ground. Oengus promises to do this, but it is his father who has to accomplish this dowry in a single night.[8]

Similarly, it is the Dagda who survives the superhuman tests imposed on him by the enemy Fomorians. He is made to eat up a porridge made of fourscore gallons of milk, goats, sheep and pigs and succeeds in returning to his people, though his belly is so distended he can scarcely stagger away, nor will his tunic cover his backside.

This element of comic vulgarity is a recurrent feature in the myths concerning the Dagda. He seems to stem from an earlier perhaps native set of myths and, apart from his great knowledge and all-inclusive prowess, is quite unlike the rest of his family. He is described in detail in 'The Intoxication of the Ulstermen':

> I saw a large-eyed, large-thighed, noble-great, immensely tall man, with a splendid grey garment about him; with seven short, black, equally-smooth cloaklets around him; shorter was each upper one, longer each lower. On either side of him were nine men. In his hand was a terrible iron staff, on which were a rough end and smooth end. His play and amusement consisted in laying the rough end on the heads of the nine, whom he would kill in the space of a moment. He would then lay the smooth end on them, so that he would reanimate them.[6]

This fantastic description from a great hilarious send-up of a comedy, shows the Dagda with his chief implement: the staff or club which has the ability to bring people alive again. In 'The Second Battle of Mag Tuiread', he is said to carry 'A wheeled fork, to carry which required the effort of eight men, so that its track after him was enough for the boundary-ditch of a province. Wherefore it is called 'The Track of the Dagda'.[6]

His ability to strike people dead and reanimate them may also be associated with the great treasure of which he is said to be the guardian: the cauldron of the Dagda, brought from Murias, from which no one came unsatisfied. As we shall see, there are other cauldrons, notably that of Bran, with whom the Dagda seems to share a similar mythos.

Bran, of British tradition, is likewise a titan among men, a giant who cannot be confined within a house, at least, not until Matholwch builds one for him. Like the Dagda, Bran seems a throwback to an earlier native mythos. His sacrificial death is on behalf of Britain, for his head is buried at the White Mount in London to ward off invasion.[17]

THE YOUNG SON

The Celts particularly venerated the Youthful God, a role typified by Mabon and Oengus mac in Dá Og. They are both gods whose mythos is inextricably associated with the passing of time and with imprisonment. The conception of Oengus is recorded in 'The Wooing of Etain'. The Dagda wanted to sleep with Boand, the wife of Elcmar, but she refused, fearing Elcmar's power. And so the Dagda sent Elcmar away on a journey and made a spell so that he would not notice the passing of time nor suffer either hunger or thirst. He would imagine that he had been away a single day, although nine months would have passed. And so the Dagda slept with Boand and she bore him a son, Oengus. This was how Oengus got his name of Mac in Dá Og: 'young the son who is conceived at dawn and born before dusk'.[6]

So it is that Oengus' begetting and birth are outside of time. In British tradition, Mabon's birth is of a similar kind, though we lack the full story, for he was 'taken from between his mother and the wall when he was three nights old',[17,73] and his whereabouts are a mystery.

Oengus is given in fosterage to Midir, believing himself to be the king's son, but he soon discovers the truth behind this protective measure to hide him from the wrath of Elcmar. Oengus goes to the Dagda, his father, to be acknowledged and given lands, but these are presently occupied by Elcmar. He bids Oengus go to Elcmar at Samhain, a time of peace, and request the kingship of Bruig na Bóinne (New Grange) for a day and night, and not to be moved until Elcmar has agreed to his judgement.

Elcmar assents to Oengus's request, but on the next day, when he comes to reoccupy the Bruig, Oengus refuses to leave and the arbitration of the matter is left to the Dagda, who judges that the land belongs to Oengus because he requested the kingship for a day and a night and 'that it is in days and nights that the world passes'.

So just as Elcmar was deceived over Oengus's conception and

birth, which took place in a single day, although really nine months by human time, so he is expelled from the Bruig by another piece of trickery. Born in no time at all, Oengus's powers extend beyond all times.

In the British story of Mabon, no such deception is apparent, for he is known only as Mabon ap Modron – Youth, son of Mother – his father being unknown. The reasons for Mabon's abduction and imprisonment seem to take place outside of time, for it only by the memory of the longest lived of animals that he is found at all.[73]

The role of Mabon or Maponus (his Gaulish title) seems mysteriously aligned with Apollo. The disappearance of Mabon may be linked to the visits of Apollo to Hyperborea – said to be located in the North and perhaps associated with the British Isles due to various mythological overlaps.

According to Diodorus Siculus, the island of Britain was supposed to be the birthplace of Leto or Latona, Apollo's mother – 'which explains why the islanders worship Apollo in particular. They are all, so to speak, priests of that god . . . One can also see in that island a huge enclosure dedicated to Apollo, and a magnificent round temple and a number of offerings.'[71] This reference has been identified as Stonehenge.

The role of the Young God is that of innocent judge and potential sacrifice. This theme is apparent in the story of Merlin Emrys, whose fate is to be sealed living in the foundations of Vortigern's tower, but who perceives the true nature of the land (Arthur), and in the story of Segda Saerlabraid, who is fated to end the wasteland of Conn's reign by being sacrificed on the plain of Tara, but is rescued by his mother.[3]

The loss and finding of the Young God follows the story-cycle of the hero who has a strange conception and an obscure upbringing, in fosterage. Pryderi, like Mabon, is stolen at birth and raised by a kindly stranger. Mabon's theft and imprisonment seem to have no rationale, but we may perceive some elements of a lost story in what remains. Lost as a baby, he emerges from his prison in Gloucester as a young, vigorous hero, ready to aid Culhwch in his impossible tasks. It is possible that Mabon has fallen into the underworld clutches of the Witches of Gloucester, who, in the story of Peredur, train and arm the hero.[72,73] There are numerous stories detailing the imprisonment and release of the Young God. In the story of Taliesin, Elphin is likewise kept in fetters and is magically released by his poet.

The relationship between the Young God and his fosterer are very close. Oengus is close to his foster-father, Midir, and, when Midir comes to stay at the Bruig, Oengus is only able to keep him there by promising to find a wife for him. It is so that the long story of Etain's transformations unfolds, for she is the wife chosen by Oengus for his foster-father.[6]

Similarly, when Manawyddan returns from the rout in Ireland, his fellow-survivor, Pryderi, offers his own mother, Rhiannon, as a possible wife for his disinherited friend, even to the extent of giving his own lands and the rulership of Dyfed into his hands.[17]

In Celtic Christian tradition, both St Bride and St Ita are associated with the fostering of Christ. As we will see, it is St Bride who takes a major role in finding the young boy when he is lost in the Temple. (See Chapter 9.)

THE OLD VEILED ONE

One of the oldest deities, perhaps a truly native goddess of Britain and Ireland who was incorporated into Celtic tradition, is the Cailleach or the Old One. She is variously named as the Grey or Blue Hag, the Gyre Carlin, Black Annis and the Hag of Beare. About her are found fragmentary stories concerning the control of the weather and the formation of mountain ranges. She is the Mountain Mother of native tradition who has submerged in Celtic story, occasionally appearing as a helper or hinderer of the hero. Like the British Ceridwen, who bears more than a trace of the Cailleach about her, she guards a cauldron into which heroes are thrust to be healed and hardened. She sometimes appears in the aspect of the Dark Woman of Knowledge, disguised as an ugly young woman who nevertheless possesses great wisdom. The fragmentary myths which remain embedded in Celtic folklore speak of her pursuit of the hero, who is often her own son. By harrying the hero she forces him to grow and develop in wisdom. Parts of her mythos have become incorporated into the Goddess of Sovereignty (see Chapter 3).

The Morrighan draws directly on the Cailleach's character. It is she whom the Dagda meets every Samhain eve in Glenn Etive. So large is she that her two feet straddle the river which is caused by her urination. Significantly, she has 'nine loosed tresses' on her head, symbolic of her association with the ninefold sisterhood of the cauldron. She and the Dagda celebrate their sexual union in that valley which is afterwards called 'the Bed of the Couple'. It is she who instructs the aos dana, the gifted people of the Tuatha de Danaan, in their struggle with the Fomorians, so that they can be magically overcome. When, by means of her wisdom, the battle is won, it is the Morrighan who proclaims the victory '. . . to the royal heights of Ireland and to its fairy hosts and its chief waters and its rivermouths'.[6]

It is so, as territorial ancestress of the land, that the Morrighan proclaims the peace, but she does not cease prophesying, going on to foretell a world in which the natural order is overtaken by unnatural disaster:

> I shall not see a world that will be dear to me.
> Summer without flowers,
> Kine will be without milk,
> Women without modesty,
> Men without valour,
> Captures without a king . . .
> Woods without mast,
> Sea without produce.[6]

Her prophetic voice echoes long down to our own times, for the Cailleach is both the giver and the taker of life and she outlives the ending of the world by renewing it within herself.

THE BRIGHT ONE

Of all the gods, Lugh has the most prominent exposure. He is the Bright One, skilful in all the arts, as we read in 'The Second Battle of Mag Tuiread', where he attempts to enter the hall of Tuatha de Danaan. The company are feasting and the gatekeeper challenges him to tell of his avowed skill. Lugh claims to be a smith, a champion, a harper, a hero, a poet, a historian, a doctor, a magician, among other things. The gatekeeper replies that they have men of these skills in their company and do not require his services, but he admits that no other possesses all these gifts, and so Lugh is admitted. He subsequently helps the Tuatha de Danaan overcome the Fomorians, killing his own grandfather, Balor, their king.[6]

Not surprisingly, Lugh is the patron of many heroes in Celtic legend, often becoming their father. Cuchulainn's parentage is exceedingly confused, but Lugh is considered to be his mystical father. Indeed many heroes exemplify the strength and abilities of Lugh to the extent that, as in Hindu belief, the hero is considered to be an avatar of the god.[95]

Lugh's British correlative, Lleu has another character altogether. Myth represents him as partially connected to the victimised Young

God or Mabon. His birth is magically, though inadvertently, contrived by his great-uncle, Math. Fostered by his uncle, Gwydion, Lleu is reared in secret and presented to his mother, Arianrhod, in order to be given a name, arms and a wife. Because of the trickery involved in his epiphany, and the shame undergone by his mother (who gives birth in full view of the court while stepping over Math's magical staff), Arianrhod refuses to name or arm him and sets on him a terrible *geasa*, that he shall have no wife of human stock. Gwydion manages to trick Arianrhod into giving Lleu a name and arms, but Math and Gwydion together have to employ magic to create a wife out of flowers for their nephew. There are no further stories about Lleu subsequent to his betrayal by and revenge upon Blodeuwedd, his wife, and it is only in the Irish legends that Lugh has his full, heroic character.[17]

THE DAUGHTERS OF BRANWEN

Within both Irish and British tradition, there are numerous goddesses, all daughters of the sea who suffer a sacrificial fate. This archetype can be identified as 'the Daughters of Branwen'. In British myth, Branwen is spoken of as one of the great ancestresses of Britain. However, since her only son is summarily killed, this title seems highly confusing. Looking deeper into the myth, we see that Branwen is the archetypal victim of dynastic marriage. Like Mabon, she innocently suffers for the sake of her country.

She is wed to the King of Ireland, Matholwch, by her brothers, led by Bran. One brother, Efnissien, is not consulted and causes much enmity between Ireland and Britain by his hostility to his sister's husband. Branwen, as a result of Efnissien's insulting behaviour to the Irish, suffers in Ireland. She is cast off and made into a kitchen drudge, although she has borne a son, Gwern. Bran hears of her disgrace and spearheads a mighty army to defeat Matholwch. Due to the intervention of Efnissien once more, Gwern is slain and the British are overcome. Bran is mortally wounded and Branwen dies of grief.[17,73]

This story is at the root of all the stories concerning the daughters of Lir: a woman exemplifies the land as the representative of the Goddess of Sovereignty, and for the sake of the land is sacrificed or dies of grief. Her long-suffering, bravely borne, has the same quality of patience and fortitude that we find in the myths of the Young God, who endures imprisonment through many aeons.

The daughters of Branwen exemplify the many disinherited queens of Celtic tradition, of whom we can cite Boudicca as the prime example. Branwen is the daughter of Llyr, the god of the sea. She shares her mythos with Creiddelad, daughter of Llydd Llaw Ereint, and Cordelia, daughter of King Lear. Creiddelad is fated never to have a husband since both Gwynn ap Nudd and Gwythyr ap Greidawl contend for her hand every May Eve until doomsday. In her person, she holds the balance of power at the cost of personal sacrifice.[17] Cordelia, on the other hand, is the upholder of the truth and refuses to flatter her aged father, Lear, but does in fact return to become Queen of Britain after his death, although she is shortly afterwards captured and commits suicide in prison.[9]

The folk story of Cap o' Rushes is derived from this composite mythos: the disinherited girl destined to marry her prince only after she has undergone the fierce purification of suffering.

Irish tradition tells of the story of the Children of Lir, of Fionnula and her brothers, enchanted into the guise of swans who suffer together an eternity of torment until they are enabled to die, transformed back into human guise, though ancient beyond telling, by a kindly monk.[14]

The myth of the daughters of Branwen embodies the enduring nature of the land itself, frequently invaded and overcome, yet abiding patiently until the time of release and vindication. For such a thing to come about, the ancestress of the land awaits the rightful king destined to avenge wrongs and recognise the features of the Goddess in the rugged face of the wasted land.

3•THE SACRED KING

CELTIC KINGSHIP

The state of the land was always a reflection of the kingly rule. If the king was in harmony with his duties and obligations, then the land flourished. If he neglected his duties, the land subsequently fell into wasteland. This theme, so familiar from the later Grail legends, arises from many Celtic stories. They date from a time when the king was sacred: neither human nor divine, but sanctioned by the elements, the manifestations of the gods of the land, and by his relationship with the Goddess of the Land, or Sovereignty.

As we shall see below, the story of Conaire mac Mess Buachalla furnishes us with interesting examples of the king's inauguration, of his obligations and duties. Conaire, like many another king, is judged by the state of his land:

> Good is his reign. Since he assumed the kingship, no cloud has veiled the sun for the space of a day from the middle of spring to the middle of autumn. And not a dewdrop has fallen from grass till midday, and wind would not touch a cow's tail until noon ... No wolf has attacked anything save one bullcalf of each byre. In Conaire's reign are the three crowns on Erin, namely, a crown of corn ears, and a crown of flowers and a crown of oak mast. In his reign, each man deems the other's voice as melodious as the strings of harps, because of the excellence of the law and the peace and the good-will prevailing throughout Erin.[6]

Spiral Mirror

We may contrast this picture with that describing the land under Conn, who has married Becuma, an Otherworldly woman outcast from the Blessed Islands: 'Conn and Becuma were a year together in Tara, and there was neither corn nor milk in Ireland during that time.'[3] Conn's druids discover that this condition is caused by Becuma's unworthiness. Conn is further told that unless he puts the woman away, Ireland will lack a third of its corn, milk and mast. This is a case where the king has put his own happiness before that of his subjects.

The seven recognised proofs of unworthiness in a king are given as follows (my translation): 'Being without truth, without law, defeat in battle, famine during his reign, dryness of cows, ruination of fruit, dearth of crops.'[64] When the king has broken his obligation to the Goddess of the Land, then the very elements of his land forsake him. During the attack on Da Derga's Hostel, his enemies' druids cause a great thirst to attack Conaire, and he asks his champion, Mac Cecht, to fetch water for him. But all the rivers and lakes of Ireland dry up.[6] The land itself refuses to aid him.

It is recognised in the *Senchus Mor* that 'there are three periods at which the world dies: the period of a plague, of a general war, of the dissolution of verbal contracts'.[27] Of the latter, 'the suspension of amity between a king and the country', is considered one of the most grievous ruptures.

THE GODDESS OF THE LAND

Celtic mythology is full of goddesses who represent the land. In Ireland, this aspect of deity became typified by Sovereignty: the goddess, or her royal, priestessly representative, in whose gift lay the sovereignty of the land. Whoever had her, had the land.

> Each year by turns,
> The chiefs held the kingdom:
> Eire, Fódla and Banbha,
> The three wives of the very strong warriors.[62]

This feature is a recurrent theme in Irish mythology where earthly kings and heroes are petitioned by the lordly ones, the people of the *sidhe*, to aid them. In return, the hero is given a faery woman as a reward and the land is wonderfully, if briefly, ruled by the heroic couple for a few years.

Sometimes a woman held the sovereignty like a Goddess, a tradition ably borne out in the historical examples of Boudicca and Cartimandua of British tradition. The Irish Maeve was Queen of Connacht for ninety-eight years, according to tradition. It was during her reign that the terrible Cattle Raid of Cooley took place and she appears as one of the greatest enemies of the hero, Cuchulainn. The strength of her sovereignty appears to derive from the land itself, for whenever she visits the island of Clothrann on Lough Ribh, she is obliged to bathe each morning in the well there – possibly to renew her youth and sovereign virtue. It is so that she is eventually slain, for Forbuidhe of the enemy Ultonians measures the distance from the mainland to the shore of this island and practises casting his sling until he can hit anything at that distance. Maeve is struck by a stone and dies.[62]

The story of Macha Red-Mane reveals an older, perhaps native pattern of monarchy, within its lines. Aodh Ruadh, Macha's father, in turn with Diothorba and Ciombarth, held the sovereignty of Ulster for seven years each. When Aodh died, Macha claimed sovereignty for herself and gave battle to all who opposed her. She won and was queen for seven years. Diothorba's sons opposed her, pleading their right of succession. Macha replied that she held Ulster by right of conquest, since she had defeated all claimants. She proceeded to marry the other claimant, Cimbaeth, making him her chief commander. Diothorba's five sons fled from her, but Macha pursued them, disguised as a beautiful leper. Each of the men desired her and she was able to lure each away and bind him. After that, the men were

27

enslaved and set to make her fort, Emain Macha, which she measured out with her cloak pin.[64]

These are rare and fragmentary stories which hint at a sacred queenship. More often the king-making stories tell of the encounter of the kingly candidate with the Goddess of Sovereignty herself who, in the form of a loathsome hag, has the kingship within her gift. Niall of the Nine Hostages becomes king because, alone of his brothers, he is willing to embrace the black *cailleach* who guards the well. Not knowing that he is undergoing a test, Niall kisses her and, in some texts, lies with her also. She turns in his arms into a beautiful maiden and announces that she is the Goddess of Sovereignty and that Niall and his heirs will be kings of Tara.[72]

This sacred union of the king and land is one of the major features of Celtic kingship and is, in one form or another, incorporated into the mystical inauguration rites of king-making.

INAUGURATION

One ancient mode of selecting the king is found in 'The Destruction of Da Derga's Hostel', where the story of Conaire is found. Conaire was the son of Mess Buachalla (the Cowherd's Fostering), really the offspring of an incestuous union between Eochaid Airem and his daughter, Etain. He gave orders that the child should be destroyed, but she smiled at her murderers and was reprieved, to live in a house having only a skylight. She is impregnated by a mysterious bird-man who comes through the roof and bids her name her child Conaire, laying on him a *geas* not to kill birds.

Shortly afterwards, Mess Buachalla is married to the king and Conaire is reared as his child. At the death of the High-King Eterscel, a great *tarbh-feis* or bull-gathering is held to determine the next king:

> A bull was killed by them and thereof one man ate his fill and drank its broth, and a spell of truth was chanted over him in his bed. Whomsoever he would see in his sleep would be king, and the sleeper would perish if he uttered a falsehood. . . . The bull-feaster, in his sleep, at the end of the night had beheld a man stark naked, passing along the road of Tara, with a stone in his sling.[6]

Conaire's fosterers wish to take him to the bull-assembly, but he delays and so it is that he meets with a flock of beautiful birds on the road to Tara which lead him on to the sea. The whole flock then turns into a troop of armed men, one of whom says: 'I am Nemhglan, king of your father's birds. You are therefore forbidden to make a cast at any bird because they are your own kind'. And he advises Conaire to proceed, according to the *tarbh-feis* vision, naked, and with a sling in his hand. It is thus that Conaire is recognised and acclaimed as king.

The *tarbh-feis* is obviously an ancient druidic form of invocation, akin to *imbas forosna* (see Chapter 5). The eating of specific meat is also recorded by Gerald of Wales, at the great marriage of the king to the land at which the king, having had intercourse with a white mare, then bathed in the broth of her flesh and ate of it. This ritual, still being enacted in twelfth-century Ulster, is akin to the Hindu rite of *asvamedha*, wherein a queen symbolically lies with a dead white stallion.[95]

So sacred is the ability to find the true king, that we find traces of the druidic vision in Adamnan's *Life of St Columba*, where Columba is visited by an angel bearing 'the glassy book of the ordination of kings', from which the saint is enabled to proclaim the next king.[1]

St Dunstan, a monk of Glastonbury Abbey who became Archbishop of Canterbury under King Edgar, was responsible for the form of the current English coronation rite. In his youth he had been expelled from court accused of 'studying the vain poems and futile stories of the pagans and of being a magician'.[50] Yet, in his coronation rite, mostly modelled on the Continental Imperial ritual, Dunstan incorporated the most fundamental of Celtic ceremonies – the wedding of the monarch to the land by means of a coronation oath and ring.

MARRIAGE TO THE LAND

Embedded in Celtic kingship custom is the understanding that the royal line is matrilineal. This may have been a native, pre-Celtic requirement: that the kingly candidate should marry a woman of the royal clan.

Tradition gives Conchobor four wives: the daughters of Eochaid Deidlech: Mumain, Eithne, Clothra and Medb. Each of these women probably represents one province of Ireland, for Medb is associated with Ulster, before becoming Connacht's queen, and Mumain's name derives from Munster. Perhaps Eithne represents Leinster and Clothra Connacht? If this is so then Conchobor is playing the game of marrying the land with a vengeance.

A remnant of the kingly marriage to the land is found in the Irish custom of the king's *droit du seigneur*, whereby he slept with each maiden before her marriage. This is one of Conchobor's *geasa* which causes embarrassment when Cuchulainn comes to wed Emer. So angry is the hero that the sages send him on a bird-gathering mission to calm him down. He returns driving all the wild animals of Ireland before him. The compromise solution to soothe the hero's wounded pride is that Conchobor is to spend the night with Emer but with his champion Fergus and his druid Cathbad in attendance.[98]

The Fianna – the Irish troops led by Fionn mac Cumhail – also retained this royal custom. Because they defended the whole of Ireland rather than one tribe, their practice of *droit du seigneur* was considered honourable reward for their services. It is this very custom that brings about their downfall. When Sgéimh Sholais (Beauty of Light), daughter of Cairpre, King of Ireland, is to wed her affianced prince, one of the Fianna demands her or else a hefty honourprice in place of this. Cairpre resolves to destroy the whole Fianna and gives battle at Gabhair (AD 283).

THE REGALIA OF THE GODDESS

The sacred obligations of the king are frequently symbolised by the empowering objects which he is set to guard. Bran the Blessed has a cauldron which gives life,[17] Cormac Mac Art is gifted with a four-sided cup of truth,[6] Nuadu has a sword whose mere wound is mortal, Gwyddno Garanhir possesses a magical food-producing hamper.[78] These symbols are emblematic of deeper concerns. While they frequently appear as the regalia of inauguration, as does the sword in the stone at the young King Arthur's acclamation, these objects are the Hallows of the land – the empowering gifts of the Goddess of Sovereignty which the king holds in trust for the whole kingdom. Guardians and heroes who seek to wield the Hallows are numerous. This understanding is the basis for the Grail quest, as I have proved elsewhere.[72]

Both Britain and Ireland have their own set of Hallows. As we saw in Chapter 1, the objects which the Tuatha de Danaan bring from the Otherworldly cities give them advantage over the rest of Ireland's inhabitants. Each Hallow is representative of a facet of balanced kingship. Britain has a tradition of Thirteen Treasures, which are said to be guarded by Merlin on the island of Bardsey. These objects, charged with power and sained with use by generations of kings, are frequently preserved in the Otherworld from whence new kings must seek to bring back their energies to recharge the land.

Those who wish to work further with the Hallows, may wish to consult *The Arthurian Tarot – a Hallowquest* (Aquarian Press, 1990) by Caitlin and John Matthews.

THE GEASA OF THE KING

With the gifts of kingship also go certain less welcome restrictions: the *geasa* (sing. *geas*) or prohibitions. Many individuals are born with a personal *geas*, like Conaire, who is not allowed to kill birds. But kingship brings further *geasa* to him. Nemhglan instructs Conaire in these:

> Your bird-reign will be noble and these shall be thy taboos:
> Thou shalt not go righthandwise round Tara and lefthandwise round Mag Brea.
> The evil beasts of Cerna must not be hunted by thee.
> Thou shalt not go out every ninth night beyond Tara.
> Thou shalt not sleep in a house from which firelight is manifest outside after sunset, and in which light is manifest from without.
> And three Reds shall not go before thee to Red's house.
> And no rapine shall be wrought in thy reign.
> And after sunset a company of one woman or one man shall not enter the house in which thou art.
> And thou shalt not settle the quarrel of thy two thralls.[6]

In 'The Destruction of Da Derga's Hostel', each of these eight *geasa* are systematically broken, thus causing Conaire's death.

Sometimes the *geasa* are associated directly with the king's relationship with the Goddess of Sovereignty. Ailill Olomm's spear has three *geasa*: it must not strike a stone, it must not kill a woman, nor must it be straightened by putting it under one's tooth. Ailill rapes Aíne ni Eoghabhal and, in retribution, she bites his ear and makes him violate his sword's *geasa*: it strikes a stone as it passes out of her and he straightens it in the forbidden way, thus causing a foulness of the breath, as well as making him blind and insane.[62]

THE MORRÍGNA

'It was a custom at that time that the king would not himself go into battle, but his smiter of battle (*túaicnid catha*) in his stead.'[87] This custom may seem very odd to us, but the sacral nature of the king meant that he did not hazard his person because his continued existence sustained the health of the land. There is also another reason for this – his land had its own protection and was defended by the Goddess herself, as the king's champion, in the person of the Morrighan.[65]

She and her sisters as the *Morrígna* – the composite threefold character of the Morrighan – frequently appear at the imminent demise of a king or hero, clustering like carrion crows over his still warm body. It is so that Badbh appears to Conaire at Da Derga's Hostel:

> As long as a weaver's beam was each of her two shins, and they were as dark as the back of a stag-beetle. A greyish woolly mantle she wore. Her lower hair reached as far as her knee. Her lips were on one side of her head. She came and put one of her shoulders against the doorpost of the house, casting the evil eye on the king.[6]

Conaire bids her prophesy for them, so she tells them that none will escape from the hostel save whatever is clutched in the claws of birds. He then asks her name. 'Cailbh' (bald), she replies. 'A bare name, that,' quips Conaire. Then she gives a list of thirty-one other names by which she is known, including that of Badbh, while standing on one leg, with one eye shut – a magical posture for such a cursing. By allowing her into the house, Conaire is made to break another of his *geasa* (see above).

As we saw in Chapter 2, the Morrighan's primacy stems from an early, pre-Celtic tradition of the Cailleach, the dark and foreboding figure who is at once the genesis and nemesis of life. She is the Goddess who defends her own, queen and scavenger of her land. The name Morrighan derives from the Celtic 'Great Queen' and it is she who is the true mystical consort of the sacred king. Remnants of this understanding are found also in British tradition, in the mythos of Rhiannon and, later, in the stories surrounding Morgan le Fay.[17,72]

THE ORACULAR HEAD

The sacral nature of the head among the Celts has long been remarked upon. In Keating's *History of Ireland*, we are given a rare glimpse into the mystery:

> It was the custom of that time that when any champion should battle another champion of great fame, he took the brain out of his head and mixed it with lime, so that he had it in the shape of a hard round ball to show at meetings and assemblies as a trophy of valour.[62]

It was foretold that the brain of Meisceadhra would avenge itself after his death, and so it was. Meisceadhra had been slain by Conchobor, who made such a trophy of his opponent's brain. It was stolen by Ceat mac Magha of Connacht who cast it at Conchobor so that it stuck irremovably in his head. On the day of the crucifixion Conchobor saw the disturbance of the elements and heard of Christ's death. He drew his sword and cut down oak-trees with it, so that the exertion killed him.[62]

In several stories, the taking of the head completes the sacrifice of the sacred king. At the disastrous siege of Da Derga's Hostel, Conaire sends his champion to fetch water for him, but when Mac Cecht returns with the water, he finds enemies hacking off the king's head. He kills the executioners and pours the long-desired and long-sought-for water down the throat of Conaire's head. His thirst quenched at last Conaire praises his champion:

> A good man Mac Cecht! an excellent man . . .
> A good warrior without, good within;
> He gives a drink, he saves a king, he doth a noble deed.[6]

Conaire is a king whose luck has run out; all his *geasa* are broken. So it is with Bran the Blessed who, in British tradition, orders his own sacrificial beheading, after having been mortally wounded.

The taking of his head marks the beginning of the modern Grail tradition, but it is Bran's own comment on kingship which is most relevant to us here: 'He who would be chief, let him make himself a bridge.' This is a statement of royal sacrifice, for Bran not only physically becomes the bridge by which his troops pass into Ireland, because of his titanic stature, but he is also a mystical bridge by virtue of his willing sacrifice. The expedition to Ireland has ended in the annihilation of the men of Britain and so Bran takes the remnant with him to the Otherworld, during which time he converses with them, teaching them all wisdom and knowledge, becoming, himself, the vessel of wisdom. The head is later buried at the White Mount, in London – the site of the present Tower of London – where it acts as a palladium in the defence of Britain.[17]

When Conall Cernach retrieves the severed head of the hero Cuchulainn, he places it upon a rock, but such is its power that it splits the stone, burying itself deep within it: a symbolic restoration of the hero into the bosom of the engendering earth.[6]

It is by the Otherworldly journey that the king becomes worthy of his title: that journey can be mystical initiation or an inter-dimensional combat.[72]

In accordance with his relationship with the land, the king was buried in the most holy part of the land. In Ireland, the burial place of kings was Bruig na Boyne. In Scotland, the Island of Iona became the place of interment. In Wales, Anglesey was the holy island. Each of these places becomes the royal enclave, the holiest earth.

THE KING'S RETINUE

Without his tribe, the king was as nothing. It was so that the king's court consisted of ten officers in constant attendance upon him, each the most worthy representative of the tribe:

> The prince to be a body-attendant on the king; the brehon to explain the customs and laws of the country in the king's presence; a druid to offer sacrifices and to forbode good or evil to the country by means of his skill and magic; a physician to heal the king and his queen and the rest of his household; a filé to compose satire or panegyric for each one according to his good or evil deeds; a seancha to preserve the genealogies, the history and transactions of the nobles from age to age; a musician to play music and three stewards with their company of attendants and cupbearers to wait on the king and attend to his wants.[62]

It is to the most important of these officers that we pass next, for without the wisdom of the druid, the eloquence of the poet and the memory of the gifted people, the king's fame would be minimal indeed.

34

4·THE GIFTED PEOPLE

SONS AND DAUGHTERS OF THE OAK

There has probably been more rubbish written about the druids than any other Celtic subject. Such is the tangled web of Classical references, revivalist speculation and wild supposition, that our common mental image of a druid is of a white-clad Father Christmas with a sickle. This is far from the truth of the matter. For the purposes of this book I have drawn, not upon Classical references, but upon the internal textual evidence of the insular Celts of Britain and Ireland.

The word *druid* (Irish *drui*, Welsh *derwydd*) is derived from the Sanskrit: *veda* – to see or know, or, possibly, from the word for oak: Gaulish *dervo*, Irish *daur*, Welsh *derw*. The words for wood and wisdom are very close: Irish *fid* and *fios* mean *trees* and *knowledge*; Welsh *gwydd* and *gwyddon* mean *trees* and *knowledgeable one*. This close connection suggests that we should think of the druid as 'a knower of the woods' or 'the wood-sage', which would give us a closer feel of what the druid really was – a seer of great knowledge, whose closeness to the natural world put him or her in the position of a walker between the worlds of humankind and the unseen worlds.[64]

Initiation in cauldron

We have been brought up to think of the druids as a priesthood but this is not borne out by the evidence. The druids were distinct from other people of the tribe by reason of their gifts. They were part of the *aos dána*, the people of art, the gifted people – although that title is more usually applied to the poetic class.

The function of the druid was to maintain what we would now call a shamanic role within the tribe. He or she – for people of either sex were druids – was the mediator, the knower, the repository of wisdom. The druids studied such abstruse matters as astrology, cosmology, physiology, theology and many other branches of learning. However, this knowledge did not make them abstract philosophers. Every part of their wisdom had to be applicable to daily life, whether it be knowing the right time for spring sowing, or the precedents of law, the prognosis of an injured limb or the nature of the gods.

Some druids specialised in certain branches of wisdom, becoming judges, prophets, teachers, poets, satirists and battle strategists as well as advisers to kings. It is unlikely that any one person fulfilled so many roles at once. For this we must look to the Otherworldly realms where the god Lugh alone is called *samildanach* – possessed of many skills (see p. 22).

We do better to think of the druid in terms of the Jewish rabbi during the diaspora: a man or woman of wisdom whose advice was sought on all matters of daily life, one who perhaps also fulfilled a craft, one who was married and had a family, one who brought the people together for common celebrations and whose word was law. Like the Hasidic rabbis who practised qabbala and were known as seers and wonder-workers, so too, the druid was a person of unusual skills.

In the druid we see the earliest form of tribal leadership – which was spiritual rather than temporal. The distinctions between king and druid are sometimes blurred in Celtic tradition. For though the king is the assumed leader of his people, it is the druid who really rules, for his or her word is law. As we have seen in Chapter 3, the king was bound about with the most fearsome *geasa*.

Our knowledge of insular druidism is necessarily curtailed by the Roman ban upon the practice of the druidic craft in Britain. Prior to the sack of the druid's centre at Anglesey in AD 64, it is likely that druids from all over the British Isles met together periodically, as the Gaulish druids are said to have done, gathering together at the Place of the Carnutes (ancient Chartres). The Continental druidic tradition suggests that Britain was the place of origination of Celtic druidism, for Gaulish druids were sent to Britain to be trained. This posits an interesting question: was druidism derived from Indo-European roots solely, or was it a dynamic fusion between the incoming Celtic peoples and the native British?

But records for British druidism are scant, due to the way in which the heartlands of Wales preserved their oral tradition for a long time, yet failed to transcribe more than a fragment of druidic lore. This left the field open to popularisers like Iolo Morgannwg (Edward Williams), whose brilliant translations of Welsh medieval verse can hardly be distinguished from his many forgeries. He is among several antiquaries and scholars of the late eighteenth century who perpetrated their personal brand of druidism upon Wales, and whose folkloric extravaganzas prop up the perfectly traditional National Eisteddfod, where poets receive the accolade of crown and chair.

The nature of druidism in Ireland varied considerably from the

Classical accounts of the Continent. This is probably for two reasons: firstly, it developed along its own lines, away from British and Continental influence; secondly, our accounts of Irish druidic practice stem from texts transcribed in Christian times. In some of these, druids are shown behaving more like the Canaanite priesthood familiar from the Bible than from true early tradition.

What did druids look like? Tacitus says that the druids and druidesses on Mona were dressed in black, but while this may be so, internal evidence of the Irish texts shows white to have been the predominant colour of both druidic robes and mantles. We are fortunate in having a detailed description of a druid, from the fantastically humorous tale, 'The Intoxication of the Ulstermen'. Each important member of the host of Ulster is described by Crom Deroil, a druid, to Cu Roi mac Dáire, who identifies each:

'I see . . . a sedate, gray-haired man in front thereof. A fair bright garment about him, with borders of all-white silver. A beautiful white shirt next to the surface of the skin; a white-silver belt around his waist; a bronze branch at the summit of his shoulder; the sweetness of melody in his voice; his utterance loud but slow . . .'

'Judicial and sage, by our conscience, is the description,' said Medb.

'Sage and judicial the person whose description it is,' said Cu Roi.

'Who, then, is he?' asked Ailill.

'Not hard to tell, Sencha the Great, son of Ailill, son of Maelchloid, from Carn Mag of Ulster; the most eloquent man of the men of earth, and the peace-maker of the hosts of the Ulstermen. The men of the world, from the rising to the setting, he would pacify with his three fair words.'[6]

Sencha is described as 'the earthly god among the Ulaid in the time of Conchobur', which is unusual enough for us to ask what exactly the status of druids really was.

The druid, as a repository for wisdom, was undoubtedly in an exalted position within the tribe. Depending on his or her ability, the druid might indeed be held in semi-divine awe.

DRUIDIC PRACTICE AND PHILOSOPHY

We have little information on how a druid was trained. From the various Celtic accounts, we find that a druid usually had one or more students attached to his retinue or household. Again, to return to our

Jewish parallel, a rabbi would often run a talmudic school for anything from a handful to a number of students. Similarly, druidic students learned from their masters and mistresses. The druidic place of learning was usually located to the north of a settlement, that being the preferred sacred direction.[64]

The method of teaching was oral instruction: long lists and correspondences were learned by heart, but this theoretical teaching was undoubtedly supplemented by practical knowledge also. The custom of a teaching dialogue is still extant in the texts, as in the following exchange, which seems very like a modern *viva voce* exam at university.

As at any modern university, where a student attends lectures by different teachers, so too, druidic candidates were frequently sent from master to mistress across the land, and often across the water to Alba or Ireland as in this example (my translation):

> Adna mac Uthidor of Connacht, was an *ollamh* of great knowledge and poetry. He had a son, Nede, whom he sent to Alba, to the school of Eochu Echbel and there he stayed until he was quite knowledgeable.
>
> Then Eochu said, 'Go home now; our joint learning should not occupy the same place, for the brilliance of your learning shows you to be an *ollamh* of knowledge'.
>
> Nede departed with his three brothers, Lugaid, Cairbre and Cruttine. They found a foxglove by the road. One of them said: 'Why is it called foxglove?' And as none of them knew why, they returned to Eochu and stayed a month with him. They took the road again and found a reed. As none of them knew why it was called so, they returned to their teacher. They left him at the end of another month and found a stalk of self-heal and not knowing why it was so called, they returned to their master's house for another month.[64]

The custom of sending children away to be taught is related to the custom of fosterage. The Scots ballad, 'The Wife of Usher's Well' tells how the carlin wife sent her three sons oversea to learn their 'grammarie' or magical arts. In a different tradition, it was so that Irish parents sent their sons to Spain to become priests during the time of Catholic proscription.

The teaching method of a learned dialogue is found in many parts of the world today, particularly in Muslim countries, but also in Ethiopia and Nepal.

THE VISION-SEERS AND SACRIFICE

In early Celtic tradition there was a distinct class known as ovates or seers. Their role seems to have been to prophesy, to observe the signs of nature and to sacrifice. Latterly, these functions – excluding sacrifice – were appropriated by the poetic class.

In the current climate of Celtic revival it may seem distasteful, if not mendacious to some, to deal with sacrifice here. However, there is no point in pulling our punches. The early Celts, along with many other peoples of the time, practised a selective form of human sacrifice.

There seem to have been four forms of sacrificial death, one for each of the elements:

hanging	= death by air
drowning	= death by water
cremation	= death by fire
burial alive	= death by earth

It is known that individual victims were slain by these methods and that their death throes became the focus of a gruesome kind of divination. The victims were usually prisoners of war, outcasts or criminals.[44]

That propitiatory sacrifice took place is evident from the numerous stories which attend the feast of Samhain (see Chapter 8). That so little mention of sacrifice is found in texts transcribed in the medieval period is really not surprising. Caesar's account of the wicker man in which were burned alive prisoners and other victims is often supposed to be a piece of Roman propaganda or else a barbarous custom of Continental Celts. However, if we look at the insular traditions, we find that stories of an iron house which is sealed and heated so as to kill the occupants are fairly widespread.

In 'The Intoxication of the Ulstermen', an ancient seer, Gabalglinde, knows of a prophecy which tells of the destruction of Ulster's great chieftains in one iron house, which can be sealed and heated from without. There are seven chains at the feet of the beds to secure the victims with. An exact replica of this house is made to destroy the Ulster host, but Cuchulainn heaves the iron house up with the help of his battle-frenzy and they escape.

So widespread is this theme, that one is tempted to think that this is a druidic story which has been partially assimilated into the literary tradition.

An iron house is an improbable construct, but so often the Celts employ metals to describe otherwise ordinary things when they wish to imply an Otherworldly shift. For instance, Manannan appears to Cormac mac Art wearing shoes of bronze. Otherworldly fortresses are walled in silver and thatched with gold or with the wings of birds. Might this iron house story have a pied meaning, perhaps signifying a cauldron? In the story of the Gundestrup cauldron we see a goddess plunging soldiers into a tub-like cauldron. We know that among Germanic tribes, the goddess Nerthus supervised such activities as the ritual drowning of her victims. The Gaulish Teutatis was propitiated by the drowning of victims in a vat. While his fellow deity, Taranis, was offered victims burned to death in a wooden vessel.[97]

But insular tradition furnishes us with other examples which are more immediate: the initiation of Taliesin and the cauldron of rebirth in which men are revived in 'Branwen'.[17]

The threefold death undergone by many characters in Celtic texts is undoubtedly connected with this teaching of sacrifice, and is also related to the 'Pledge of the Elements', which call upon the air, water and earth to obliterate the unfaithful oath-maker.

Latterly, the role of ovate was concerned solely with far-vision and prophecy. We see the figure of Merlin as related to this function, when he prophesies for Vortigern.[9] Prophetic or precognitive vision certainly arose out of the ovate living in close harmony with the elements. Some Celtic hermits were later famed for their miraculous visionary insights, and this is not surprising, living as they did in complete isolation in the heart of the forest.

Poets also shared something of this precognitive skill. As the druidic system fell into decay, it was the *fili*, the visionary poets, who preserved the lore of the ovate and prophet.

The function of the ovate or prophet is one still very much associated with people of Celtic extraction today, many of whom possess 'the second sight'.

BREHONS

All the *aos dána* preserved a sense of natural justice, but a particular class of judges, the brehons, were appointed to oversee the courts of judgement. That we know so much about their work is due almost entirely to the *Seanchus Mor*, which preserves the ancient laws of Ireland in great detail. These laws were still in use until the British judicial system was imposed. The circuits which Celtic *brehons* went upon are still a feature of the current British judiciary. The *brehon* settled disputes, arbitrated and gave judgements and punishments and fines.

Every person and thing had their honour price: the indemnity which had to be paid in the case of accidental or purposeful injury. The first indemnity to be so judged was in the time of Partholón when he left his wife alone with a servant and they committed adultery.

Math ap Mathonwy seems to have had druidic training as a judge, since he proclaims that Gwydion and Gilfaethwy, who have raped his foot-holder, Goewin, should be exiled from court. Math forbids anyone to feed or shelter them, and they are eventually forced back to their judge to make compensation. It is then that Math strikes them with his druidic wand and changes them into wild beasts for three years, to mate and breed until they have cleared their guilt. Goewin becomes Math's wife.[17]

Similarly, Manawyddan acts with the skill of a judge when he prepares the gallows to hang Llwyd's wife who, in the shape of a mouse, has been stealing his crops by night.[17]

The use of divination as the basis of a judgement appears rarely in the *Seanchus Mor*. This method is called *crannchur* or 'casting the woods'. If there is some doubt about the innocence of the one accused of murder, then,

> the lots are cast in this manner: three lots are put in, a lot for guiltiness, a lot for innocence, and the lot of the Trinity. This is enough to criminate or acquit them. If it be the lot of the Trinity that came out, it is to be put back each time until another lot comes out.[27]

The same method is utilised to determine which animal has caused damage to property or, in the case of an injured bee, to which hive it belongs so that compensation can be given to its owner.

Crannchur may or may not have originally utilised *oghams*, but we have no textual evidence to prove this. See Chapter 5.

There seems to be a distinct preference for the judgement to be transferred to the power of the elements themselves. In the case of incest, the punishment was to be set adrift in an open boat with no oar, sail or rudder. If the party survived, then the elements had given their judgement. It is so that Mordred survives his exposure in an open boat to become King Arthur's nemesis.[75]

THE WOMEN OF ART

Although many of the examples cited here detail instances of male druids or poets, the full range of the professional arts were open to women also.

The *bánfáith* or medium whom Medb consults, Fedelm, was the prophetess of Cruachan, but she gives a dismal augury to the queen as to the outcome of the battle: 'I see it red, I see it bloody.'[30]

There is a remarkable story concerning the superior prowess of a *bánfili* or poetess in *Cormac's Glossary* which has supernatural elements within it that are akin to both the *immrama* or wonder voyages and to the long-established tradition of 'the provoker of strife' in Celtic tradition.[72]

The great poet, Senchan, made a holiday trip to the island of Mann with his retinue of fifty poets and students. As he was about to disembark, a hideous youth hailed the boat from the shore and demanded to be let on board, saying, 'I am more profitable to you than that foolish, mighty set that is with you.' Senchan let him on board, but so outrageous was his behaviour that he nearly overturned the boat. The poets all called out: 'A monster has beset you, Senchan, and it will be the only living thing to come ashore with you.' Whereafter, Senchan was surnamed Torpeist.

When they landed, they saw there an old woman gathering seaweed. They noted that, though her clothes were ragged and her appearance famine-thin, she had 'signs of rank on her feet and hands'. She was none other than a great poetess, the daughter of Ua Dulsaine, master-poet of north-west Munster. Her brother had been seeking her for many years, but she was lost to him.

When she saw the poets, she asked who they were. 'Worthy are the ones you are asking,' they said, and presented her to Senchan.

'Will you be humble, Senchan?' she asked, and began a poetic combat with him.

> 'Tribulation is not my accustomed lot,
> My only comfort is the blistered sea-wrack . . .

'What is the next half-quatrain?'

Senchan and all his poets were dumbfounded. Then the hideous youth leapt up and said, '*Cailleach* leave Senchan alone, and challenge me, for none of this family should address you.' And he was able to supply the next two lines (my translation):

> 'From the skin of Mann's rock
> Much salt has been made.'

43

Then she said,

> 'What man thinks on me daily,
> For my two ears burn me greatly? . . .'

Again the hideous youth completed the lines:

> 'Who but Mac Ua Dulsaine, the artist
> From Liac of Tursaige Thúill.'

Then even Senchan recognised who she was and bore her home in his ship. But when they reached Ireland, the hideous youth was already on the shore, only now he was transformed into the fairest young man in the world.[25]

This story turns round two concepts: that a poet should be able to cap any line quoted to him after having only heard it once before; and that the poetess gathering seaweed has a father called Ua Dulsaine. A form of seaweed, called dulse, is still gathered and eaten today. The hideous youth who transforms himself into a fair young man is the spirit of poetry himself: though the art is hard and disagreeable at first, whoever applies himself to it will find it beautiful and satisfying.

When Midir takes Etain to his home, Oengus warns him against Midir's wife, Fuamnach, who is described as, 'a woman of dreadful sorcery, a woman with all the knowledge and skill and power of her people'. Fuamnach was of the Tuatha de Danaan and trained with Breseal the druid before her marriage to Midir. Fuamnach's jealousy of Etain causes her to enchant her rival. She strikes Etain with a rod of scarlet rowan wood and changes her into a pool of water, a worm, a fly and, lastly, she conjures a strong wind to blow the fly away. Fuamnach is a real *bean-druí* or druidess of the Tuatha de Danaan.[8]

Two female satirists appear in the mythic stories. Lebharcham becomes foster-mother of the tragic Deirdruí while Richis, foster-mother of Crimthann, attempts to revenge her son's death on Cuchulainn in 'The Intoxication of the Ulstermen'. Knowing of Cuchulainn's modesty at the sight of naked women, she confronts him naked so that he averts his gaze and bids Crimthann attack. However, Loegaire, Cuchulainn's charioteer, kills Richis by throwing a great rock at her.[8]

The fostering of heroes was an especial task of the women of art. Fionn's own fostermothers were two women-warriors and a druidess.[90]

THE FORGE OF LEARNING

The training of the poet was a formidable course of study, lasting at least twelve years. We are fortunate in possessing the seven grades of poets and their curriculum.

In the first year, the elementary or preparatory grade, the student studied elementary grammar and learned twenty stories. In the second year, he increased his learning of *oghams*, began philosophy and poetry and memorised ten more stories. The third year built upon this programme, adding more stories, *oghams* and the intricacies of assonantal versification. In the fourth year, he learned the *Bretha Nemed*, or Law of Privileges, as well as more poems and stories. The fifth year examined the uses of grammar and built upon the foregoing curriculum. In the sixth year, he learned the Secret Language of Poets, and forty-eight more poems.

In the seventh, eighth and ninth years, the poet was called, *anrúth* or noble stream; 'a stream of pleasing praise issuing from him, and a stream of wealth to him.' He learned the *Brosnacha*, the collections of teachers, the styles of poetic composition, prosody, glosses, *teinm laeghda, imbas forosna, dichetal do chennaib* (see Chapter 5), the *Dindsenchas*, poetic forms, and became master of 175 tales (including the 80 stories already learned).

The tenth, eleventh and twelfth years saw his establishment as an *Ollamh*, or doctor. This position has three grades: *eces* – man of learning, *fili* – poet, and *ollamh*. He perfected further poetic forms and composition, learned 100 poems of the *anamuin* genre, restricted to *ollamhs*, as well as 120 Orations, the four arts of poetry, and became master of 350 stories in total.[61] Such an education was tedious and yet fulfilling. The manner in which poetic schools were run may help us posit how druids were trained, since we have little or no textual evidence for this. The poetic schools were formed about one teacher and his attendants, with the addition of auxiliary visiting poets who also acted as examiners. The head of such a school was probably an *ard-ollamh*, or chief poet, maintained by his patron.

While we can discern a distinct hereditary succession of occupation, poets could be trained from most classes, the chief qualifications being a strong memory and a facility with language. Much of the learning was by rote and, in order to strengthen the memory and to dispense with unnecessary distractions, the student's accommodation was spartan in the extreme.

We find from descriptions of later bardic schools that much of the study was in total darkness:

> The reason of laying the Study aforesaid in the Dark was doubtless to avoid the Distraction which Light and the variety of Objects represented thereby commonly occasioned. This being prevented, the Faculties of the Soul occupied themselves solely upon the Subject in hand, and the Theme given; so that it was soon brought to some Perfection according to the Notions or Capacities of the Students.[43]

This method of study was still commonly practised by poets in the Western Highlands in the eighteenth century. They were said to

> . . . shut their Doors and Windows for a Day's time, and lie on their backs with Stone upon their Belly, and Plads about their Heads, and their eyes being cover'd they pump their Brains for Rhetorical Encomium or Panegyrick; and indeed they furnish such a Stile from this Dark Cell as is understood by very few.[43]

This may sound fantastically uncomfortable, but those who had committed their lives to this tradition longed after it with supernatural affection. So eloquent were the teachers that, says one poem, the students thereafter found the song of the cuckoo harsh and unappealing. The unknown poet who penned the following lines was writing in a time when the poetic schools were outlawed, some time after the seventeenth century:

> The three forges wherein I was wont to find mental delight, that I cannot visit these forges wears away the armoury of my mind.
>
> The house of memorising of our gentle lads – it was a trysting place of youthful companies – embers red and shining, that was our forge at the first.
>
> The house of reclining for such as we, the university of art, poetic cell that kept us from beguilement, this was the great forge of our trained anruth.
>
> The house of the critic of each fine work of art was the third house of our three forges, which multiplied the clinging tendrils of knowledge, wherein the very forge of science was wont to be.
>
> Three sanctuaries wherein we took rank, three forges that sustained the loving companies of artists, houses that bound comrades together.[43]

To such men and women who underwent this training, their mother was memory, sustaining and nourishing them, preserving a great tradition which descends, only fragmentedly, to our own day.

THE MOTHER OF MEMORY

In Irish the word 'to teach' also means 'to sing over', and this sums up the oral tradition: one which is still employed in parts of the world today. The Koran is still learned orally in this manner, the imam singing and his pupils reciting. This dialogue brought the student to deep knowledge and was yet another link in the golden chain of tradition.

When it is asked 'What has preserved the *Seanchus Mor?*' the answer is a telling one: 'The joint memory of two seniors, the tradition from one ear to another, the composition of poets, the addition from the law of the letter, strength from the law of nature; for these are the three rocks by which the judgements of the world are supported.'[27]

It is interesting that both the oral, pagan tradition (the law of nature) and the literary, Christian tradition (the law of the letter) are both invoked here.

Whether oral or literary, the tradition has relied on the strength of memory and the living links in the chain of transmission. In 'The Colloquy of the Two Sages', the *fili*, Nede, gives us an insight into the genealogy of memory:

> I am the son of Poetry,
> Poetry, son of Reflection,
> Reflection, son of Meditation,
> Meditation, son of Lore,
> Lore, son of Research,
> Research, son of Great Knowledge,
> Great Knowledge, son of Intelligence,
> Intelligence, son of Comprehension,
> Comprehension, son of Wisdom,
> Wisdom, son of the three gods of Dana.[28]

This genealogy of memory is easy to gloss, since the ancestress of this line is none other than Brigit herself (my translation):

> It is this Brigit who is poetess or the wise-woman whom the poets worship, because of her great and wondrous protection. It is for this reason that she is called the Goddess of Poets, she whose sisters are Brigit the healer, and Brigit the smith. These goddesses are the three daughters of the Dagda. The three sons of Brigit the poetess are Brian, Iuchar and Uar, the three sons of Bres, son of Elatha. Brigit the poetess, daughter of the great Dagda, being their mother.[64]

47

Brigit is the patron of all the *aos dána*, the true mother of memory, who fosters the creative and magical arts. It is perhaps a late remembrance of her powers to keep knowledge safe from all scathe that the West Highlanders recited their 'Genealogy of Bride' which, while it tells of St Bride rather than the Goddess of Poets, still has talismanic power to preserve life:

> Every day and every night
> That I say the genealogy of Bride,
> I shall not be killed, I shall not be harried,
> I shall not be put in a cell, I shall not be wounded . . .
> No fire, no sun, no moon shall burn me,
> No lake, no water, nor sea shall drown me.[35]

5·THE SILVER BRANCH

THE SILVER BRANCH

The poets or *fili* were closely in touch with the Otherworld. This much is clear from the shamanic regalia of their office, chief among which was the musical branch which they carried. A chief poet, or *ollamh*, was entitled to a gold branch, an *anruth* carried a silver one and all the lower classes of poet were entitled to a bronze branch. These branches had bells which tinkled as the poet rode along, or which chimed as he walked into the hall.[61]

This concept of the musical branch seems central to Celtic tradition. This branch was analogous to the branch of the Otherworldly tree which grew in the Blessed Islands of the West on which sat the Birds of Rhiannon. Whoever heard them remained in a timeless state, as do Bran and his Noble Company in the story of Branwen.[17] In 'The Settling of the Manor of Tara', we read of Trefuilngid Tre-eochair (T. of the Three Keys or Saplings), a great Otherworldly being of titanic size, who comes to Tara bearing in his hands a branch with three fruits upon it: nuts, apples and acorns.[4] This concept of the ever-fertile Otherworldly tree is closely related to the vitality of poetic creation and tradition, which is continually renewed in every generation, passing from master to student.

The magical regalia of the poet was not complete without his

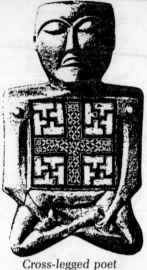

Cross-legged poet

tuigen, or bird-mantle. This was a feathered cloak, very similar to those still worn by the Maoris of New Zealand. The *tuigen* was made of 'the skins of birds white and many-coloured . . . from the girdle downwards, and of mallards' necks and of their crests from the girdle upwards to the neck'.[25] Other sources say that the *tuigen* was predominantly of small songbird's feathers, but that the neck was made of the skin and feathers of the swan, with the swan's neck hanging down behind like the tippet on a modern university gown.

Other stories tell of druids, such as Mog Ruith, wearing ceremonial bullshides and donning headdresses of birds' feathers. All these descriptions give us a picture of a professional class who were firmly rooted in their original native tradition which synthesised magic, shamanism and originative memory techniques.

POWER OF THE WORD

The Fomorians fought against Partholón with one foot, one hand and one eye – a typical magical posture of cursing. In 'The Destruction of Da Derga's Hostel', a monstrous woman comes to ask hospitality and when asked her name, she recites a list of thirty-one names while standing on one foot and with one outstretched. She curses the assembly with the curse of Macha (see p. 11), which renders the company as weak as a woman in childbed for nine nights.

Similarly Lugh adopts this posture in his battle against the

Fomorians: 'Lugh took upon himself the form of an old woman all twisted on one side, with one leg, one hand, one eye, and made a circuit about the respective armies, prophesying disaster and death on all the Fomorians, while encouraging the men of Ireland.'[8]

The magical facility was not reserved for druids or ovates, but was incidental to the poet's practice. This may seem strange to us, accustomed as we are to the present status and practice of poetry in our society, but the roots of poetry are inextricably entwined with the mantic arts of invocation, memory and the inner realms. The high arts of poetry as practised by the *fili*, the master-poets, brought them into a similar alignment with the wisdom practised by the druids. The sheer weight of training, of honing the memory and refining concentration, brought the *fili* to a pitch of magical dexterity. These skills were normally employed in evoking and portraying the ancestral stories of the tribe, in praising tribal leaders and heroes, in aligning their listeners with the Otherworld. But these powers could also function in other, less pleasant ways.

The poet's chief power was primarily that of the word. Within the limits of natural justice, the poet was at liberty to make a satire if his fee had been unlawfully withheld or if his person had been subjected to insult or dishonour. Since the poet's prime function was to uphold honour by means of praise, or the recitation of ancestral wisdom and story which redounded to the tribal honour, his words were carefully noted and his satires feared.

Sometimes the effect of a satire is brought about in other ways. The infant Taliesin was able to wreak havoc on the dignity of Maelgwn Gwynnedd's poetic company when they went up to the king to demand their fee; as they passed Taliesin he played 'blerwm, blerwm' on his lips with a finger and they promptly ignored him. However, when they stood before the king, all they could say, similarly, was 'Blerwm, blerwm.' Amazed at their behaviour, the king demanded to know if they were drunk, but the bards were forced to admit that Taliesin had caused them to act thus.[17,78]

A poet could create magical changes in the landscape or in beasts, making both barren, or his words could cause blisters on the face of his enemy. His satires might be no worse than a fierce lampoon which would be gleefully spread by gossips and so work its eventual result: to hold up anyone who slighted him in a dishonourable and mocking light.

So then, the powers of the poets in Celtic society was proverbial but their demands and menaces eventually led to their virtual dissolution in the sixth century.

At the convention of Drum Ketta in AD 574, King Aed Mac Ainmirech and many of the kings and chieftains of Ireland, resolved to banish all poets from the country. The occasion of this decision was forced by a poet demanding of King Aed his *roth croi* or royal wheel-brooch, which was an heirloom passed down through the kingly line, not a mere piece of jewellery such as a poet might demand for his fee. The situation was salvaged by the intervention of St Columba, who returned from his self-imposed exile in Iona to arbitrate on the poet's behalf. A stricter set of laws regulated the behaviour, payment and work of poets as a result of this. We note that this dispute concerned only the *fili* – the poet-masters – not the itinerant bards.

THE POWER OF THE ELEMENTS

The manipulation of the elements, or weather-witching, was a druidic skill employed to great effect during wartime, as we have seen above, or in incidents of enchantment.

The druidical wind was raised by the Tuatha to repel the Milesians.[15] A similar wind is raised by Taliesin to free Elphin from his prison.[17]

Cloaks of invisibility looking like grey clouds are quite common. Caswallawn has such a cloak and with it he raises a magical fog to overcome the army of Britain when Bran is absent in Ireland.[17] Cu Roi ma Daire, the magical ruler of Munster, is very much the 'man in the grey mantle' also, and with his druidic skills, he is enabled to bring out Blanaid from the otherworldly fortress of Manainn.[62]

Druids also set up magical hedges between armies and dry up rivers and lakes, in order to overcome the enemy. Hills are also laid flat. And so every kind of elemental persuasion was used to change the outcome of battle.

DIVINATION

Without doubt, one of the duties of the ovates or *fáithi* (sing. *fáith*), the seers of the Celtic world, was to divine the affairs of humankind from close observation of nature. O'Currey sites a small tract on divination housed in Trinity College, Dublin. One part of this ms. deals with dreams. The entries and their associative interpretations are terse and uninformative, but they do give a flavour of the kind of augury to be expected: 'A dead King denotes shortness of life. A King dying denotes loss. A King captured alive denotes evil. A brilliant Sun denotes blood. A dark Sun denotes danger. Two Suns in one night, disgrace. The Sun and Moon in the same course, battles.[88]

Augury by means of birds' song or flight was by no means a practice restricted to the Celts but birds figure largely in Celtic divination. From the same tract quoted above, comes the following extract concerning divination by croaking of raven:

> If the Raven croaks over a closed bed within the house, this denotes that a distinguished guest, whether lay or clerical, is coming to you. . . . If it be a layman that is to come, it is *bacach! bacach!* the raven says. But if it is to be a man in holy orders, it is *gradh! gradh!* it says; and it is far (i.e. late) in the day that it croaks. If it be a soldier or a satirist that is coming, it is *grog! grog!* or *grob! grob!* that it croaks; and it is behind you that the Raven speaks, and it is from the direction the guests are to come.[88]

Divination of the future, or prophecy, was inextricably bound up with the favourable or unfavourable nature of days. This kind of prescience is often employed in the stories to do with the conception of children or with the rites of passage. When Cathbadh's students ask him one day what that particular day is good for, he tells them that whoever takes arms on that day will be famous among all the men of Ireland and will have stories told about him for ever. Hearing this, the 9-year-old Cuchulainn immediately sets about becoming a man on that day.[8]

The story of Fiachiadh Muilleathan's conception relates how Moncha, his mother, consulted a druid about the birth of her son. He would become a king, said the druid, if he was born the next day, but would only be a druid if she gave birth that very day. She took herself to the river Suir and there sat on a stone resisting the child's birth until the following day, dying immediately. Fiachaidh was called Muilleathan (Broad Brow) because of the flattening of his head on the stone.[62]

The conception of Conchobor tells of how Nessa asked the nature of the hour from Cathbadh, the druid. When he replied that it was a good hour for the begetting of a king upon a queen, Nessa immediately took the druid inside with her and so Conchobor was conceived.[95]

THE THREE ILLUMINATIONS

There were three forms of divination employed by the druidic and poetic class. Two of these were outlawed by St Patrick, because they involved invocation of pagan gods. Very few examples of these methods have survived, but we can briefly glimpse some of their power. They are known as *imbas forosna, teinm laída*, and *díchetal di chennaib*. We are told that after Fionn ate of the salmon of wisdom (cf. p. 67), he thereafter had 'the three qualifications of a poet'.[90]

Imbas Forosna or 'The Inspiration of the Masters' (or 'of Tradition') is termed 'Illumination by the Palm of the Hand' by O'Currey. (Modern Irish: *iomas* = inspiration, *foroideas* = tradition, elementary instruction.) The poet or druid would chew upon the flesh of certain animals – such as a bull, cat, dog, etc. – and, after ritual invocations, would cast himself into a sleep of incubation during which he would receive a true augury. It would seem that this method gave access to the wisdom guarded by the totemic beast thus consumed.

As we have seen, the *tarbh feis* was a means of discovering the next king, according to 'The Destruction of Da Derga's Hostel'.[6] In *Cormac's Glossary*, we hear how *imbas forosna* was further accomplished by the poet lying in a darkened room, with the palms of his hands over either eye, crossways across his face.[25] This is an instance of magical posture which is not unknown in other systems of meditation, since it acts as a total blotting out of light which might interfere with the inner vision. A form of *imbas forosna*, without the preliminary meal of meat, was practised as a method of poetic composition as late as the eighteenth century in the Western Highlands of Scotland, the poet lying in a darkened room with a blanket over him while he struggled with his poem.[100]

Teinm Laeghda or 'The Cracking Open of the Poem' might be further translated as 'Poetic Analysis' or, as O'Currey has it, 'The Illumination of Rhymes'. (Modern Irish: *teinm* = breaking, cracking, gnawing, analysis; *laoídh* = poem.) An example of this method is given in a story below. Its chief exponent in Irish tradition, is Fionn mac Cumhail himself who possessed the thumb of knowledge. He had only to put this in his mouth and he would intuit what needed to be known.[90]

Teinm Laeghda seems to have followed a set pattern of ritual invocations again. In the story below, we find that Fionn allows the act of entering into poetic inspiration to evoke the answer. This technique seems to work by means of conjugating or analysing a given situation poetically, until an answer is intuited.

Dichetal do Chennaib, 'Composing on One's Finger-Ends', or, as O'Currey has it, 'Great Extempore Recital' is the least documented method of divinatory inspiration. It has been suggested by Robert Graves that the hand was used as a mnemonic, each joint pertaining to an ogham letter.[53] While this theory is persuasive, we may not necessarily equate it with *Dichetal do Chennaib*, which seems to have more in common with psychometry. Some texts speak of a poet's ability to touch someone with his staff or to pick up an object and, by means of ritual invocation to discover the history of that person or object.

An instance of this is found in 'The Exile of the Sons of Uisnech', where the hosts of Ulster are being served by the wife of Fedlimid. She is pregnant and as she passes through the hall, the child cries out in her womb. At this shriek the company arises in fright, but the woman asks the druid, Cathbadh, to give her an augury about this cry. Laying a hand on her belly, Cathbadh pronounces:

> It is a woman who hath given that shriek,
> Golden haired, with long tresses, and tall,
> For whose love chieftains shall strive . . .
> O Deirdruí! thou art great cause of ruin;
> Though famous, and fair and pale:
> Before Fedlimid's daughter shall part from life,
> All Ulster shall wail her deeds.[6]

A ninth-century charm against illness gives this charm: 'Insert the two fingers that are next to the little finger into your mouth, each of them apart';[90] this may also be part of this technique.

A story which shows a combined instance of *Teinm laeghda* and divination by ogham in action, is found in the Fionn cycle.

Fionn left his wife to go hunting. Lomna, his faithful fool, observed the woman's friendliness with Cairpre, one of Fionn's warriors. She bade Lomna keep silence on this matter, which he did reluctantly. Unable to keep Fionn in ignorance, Lomna shaped a quadrangular wand and cut the following upon it in ogham letters: 'An alder stake in a palisade of silver; a sprig of hellebore in a bunch of cresses; the willing husband of an unfaithful wife among a select band of tried warriors; heath upon the bare hill of Ualainn in Luighne.' He then left the wand where Fionn would find it.

Fionn's otherworldly knowledge helped him understand this obscure message and, in order to cover her tracks, Fionn's wife bade her lover kill Lomna. The fool's headless body was shortly found and the Fianna asked Fionn to divine whose body it was and how he met his end. Fionn put his thumb into his mouth and 'spoke through the power of *Teinm Laeghda*:

> "He has not been killed by people –
> He has not been killed by the people of Laighné –
> He has not been killed by a wild boar –
> He has not been killed by a fall –
> He has not died on his bed, – Lomna!

This is Lomna's body," said Fionn. "And enemies have carried away his head."'[88]

The 'Illumination by Rhymes' here demonstrates the dead man's name spontaneously springing to Fionn's lips. It is possible that this method of divination followed a set form, unlike *dichetal do chennaib*, which seems to have been a more analeptic skill, possibly akin to psychometry.

The obscurity of the ogham is no trouble to Fionn, who successfully determines, by means of a phrase ogham, that the alder stake in a palisade of silver denotes his own wife in her court; a sprig of hellebore in a bunch of cress means that her intentions are unwholesome; that the woman is his own wife and the place of her lover's assignation are conveyed by Lomna's message. The story continues interestingly:

Fionn let loose his hounds, who tracked to where Cairpre was cooking a fish on a stone. Lomna's head was staked nearby. Three times did Cairpre divide the fish, giving nothing to the head, which said:

'A speckled white-bellied salmon bursts forth from spawn under the sea.'

'You have divided a share at the second division. A better division would be made by a drunken servant. I would like a piece of the stomach. The fianna will hate Luighne for this!'

At this, Cairpre bade his men throw the head away, but it said:

'The stake relates that a champion was running with his battle-spear at their first coupling. Ye will be like many pieces or several fragments. Fionn will light the Luighne with much fire.'[90]

Fionn then approached and killed Cairpre, as Lomna prophesied.

Lomna also seems to employ a kind of *teinm laída*, his oracular head performing much the same function as Bran the Blessed's.

Each of the techniques is obscure and barely understood by the clerics who wrote the stories down. They have a tendency to lump all three together in an arbitrary way. Their true purpose was allied to the poet's magical abilities. The rigorous training sensitised the poet to observe and identify the essence of a person, thing or situation in ways that seem miraculous to us, but which, like all divination, was based on firm observation and training.

Table 5:1   The Ogham Alphabet

Letter	Irish Name	Tree	Welsh Name
B	beith	birch	bedwen
L	luis	rowan	cerdinen
F	fearn	alder	gwernen
S	saille	willow	helygen
N	nuin	ash	onnen
H	huathe	hawthorn	draenen wen
D	duir	oak	derwen, dar
T	tinne	holly	celynnen
C	coll	hazel	collen
Q	quert	apple	afal
M	muinn	vine	gwinwydden
G	gort	ivy	eiddew, iorwg
NG	ngetal	broom/fern	eithin/rhedynen
STR	straif	blackthorn	draenen ddu
R	ruis	elder	ysgawen
A	ailm	fir/pine	ffynidwydden/pinwydden
O	onn	gorse	eithin
U	ur	heather	grug
E	edhadh	aspen	aethnen
I	ido	yew	ywen
EA	ebhadh	aspen	aethnen
OI	oir	spindle	piswydden
UI	uileand	honeysuckle	gwyddfid
IO	iphin	gooseberry	eirin Mair (plums of Mary)
(AE)	phagos	beech	ffawydden

OGHAM AND WOOD WISDOM

The Ogham alphabet has caused a good deal of controversy among scholars of this century. As we have already noted, the Celts did not use writing to record their traditions and stories. However, the ogham alphabet, given in Table 5:1, seems to have been used in two ways: as a method of inscription on pillar stones, and as a method of memorising and containing a vast compendium of complex and abstruse knowledge. One may well call it the Celtic Theatre of Memory.

Similar methods of memorisation have been used by Classical writers as well as medieval philosophers. They would imagine a large building, well-known to them, and people it with images in order to fix in memory certain associations and recollections. The ogham alphabet had a similar use. But it is its magical usage which concerns us most here.

The straight strokes were incised along the edge of a stone or billet of wood. It would be hard to imagine a more unwieldy way of recording information than ogham, and this was clearly not its prime use. Pillar-stones record and commemorate the names of famous people or boundary points. Ogham staves had other poetical and magical uses. They were suitable for sending brief, telegrammic messages or else powerful spells. The internal evidence of Celtic texts gives terse testimony to its real uses.

This list is derived from *Auraicept na Eces*,[5] with the modern Welsh equivalents given; it may differ from other lists in small detail. The doubling of E and EA for aspen occurs throughout this text.

Irish tradition also designated the different trees under the criteria of Chieftain, Peasant, Shrub or Herb trees. Whoever felled or damaged trees was liable to varying degrees of fines and penalties under the law, according to which tree was involved.[27]

Chieftain Trees: oak, hazel, holly, apple, ash, yew, fir
Peasant Trees: alder, willow, birch, elm, hawthorn, aspen, quicken
Shrub Trees: blackthorn, elder, spindle, test-tree, honeysuckle, bird-cherry, white-hazel
Herb trees: gorse, heather, broom, bog-myrtle, rushes.

The mythology of the ogham alphabet's invention is as follows:

> In the time of Bres, son of Elatha, King of Ireland it was invented. Its person Ogma, son of Elatha . . . Now Ogma, a man well skilled in speech and in poetry, invented the Ogham. The cause of its invention, as a proof of his ingenuity, and that this speech should belong to the learned apart, to the exclusion of rustics and herdsmen.[86]

The very first use of Ogham was sent as a warning to Lugh, son of Ethliu, saying, 'Thy wife would be carried away from thee into faeryland or into another country, unless birch guard her. On that account, moreover, b, birch, takes precedence, for it is in birch that Ogham was first written.'[5]

In 'Tochmarc Etain' (The Wooing of Etain), the druid Dálán discovers Etain's hiding-place by cutting four wands of yew, and writing oghams upon them. He subsequently finds, by this method, the *eochra écsi* (keys of divination).[8]

There are fragmentary evidences for the use of *ogham* for divination, as we have already encountered in the discussion of the brehons' use of *crannchur* or 'casting the woods'. Similar expressions, implying the throwing of inscribed pieces of wood, are found in other Celtic traditions; Breton *prenn-denn*, Cornish *teulel pren*. The Welsh word *coelbren* is clearly from the same general root meaning.[63]

With a consideration of *coelbren*, we enter a shady area. This system of inscription was apparently invented on the spot by the ninth-century Welshman, Nemnivius, who was challenged by a Saxon with the Briton's lack of a written language. The subsequent history of *coelbren* seems to have been similarly dishonourable, since it formed part of the dubious druidic writings of Iolo Morgannwg, and was further obscured. A quadrangular frame, called a *Peithynen*, or elucidator, was supposed to be employed for divination; the *coelbren* symbols inscribed on their slats were able to move about like slats on an abacus, one imagines, according to this tradition. Such a use is not impossible, though hard to envisage. The system of *koelbren* has been recently revived by Kaledon Naddair, who has utilised it in an original and shamanistic way.[83]

Many people have assumed that Ogham and Runic inscriptions must derive from each other, but this is not so. The former is a Celtic method, the latter a Scandinavian one. Both are concerned with arcane knowledge, both are under the patronage of gods of word-wisdom.

In Irish tradition, there is mention of poetic tablets, though these seem to be more in keeping with the Coligny Calendar than with methods of divination. The story is told about the love and tragic deaths of Baile and Ailinn. Through Baile's grave grew a yew which had a semblance of Baile's head at its top. Through Ailinn's grave grew an appletree with the semblance of her head upon it. At the end of seven years, the poets and seers of Ulster cut down the tree to make poetic tablets on which to inscribe the visions, festivals, loves and customs of their people. In a similar manner, the poets of Leinster cut down Ailinn's tree and made poetic tablets. On one Samain when all the *aos dana* were assembled, the King, Art mac

Conn, asked to see these tablets. As he held them in either hand, one tablet jumped up and 'they reunited like honeysuckle about a branch, so that no-one could separate them again.'[64]

Table 5:2 gives a list, not of hard and fast correspondences, but suggested uses of bird ogham, colour ogham, and fortress ogham. It will be seen that the initial letter defines the grouping. Other oghams work on the principle of dividing the alphabet into fives: the B group, the H group, the M group, the A group. e.g. Bull ogham gives bulls for the B group – b = 1 bull, l = 2 bulls, f = 3 bulls etc., the H group is oxen, the M group is bullocks, the A group is steers. A similar form is used for dogs, cows, bodies of water, etc.

Some oghams were created silently by gesture: foot, nose or palm oghams were performed by placing the fingers of the hands across, respectively, the shinbone, the nose or the palm of the hand to indicate the shape of the strokes. In this way, poets could sign to each other without the unlearned knowing what they said, thus preserving the secret brotherhood of poets.

The late Sean O'Boyle argued persuasively that one of the ogham alphabets known as *aradach Fionn*, or Fionn's Ladder (see Fig. 5:1), was a method of harp tablature. Before the formalisation of musical notation, various methods of tablature were used to record the value of musical notes. O'Boyle argues that the twenty ogham characters each represent a note on a twenty-string harp. Since this number of strings is sufficient to accompany by, such an instrument could have served as a practice harp.[86]

THE BATTLE OF THE TREES

Modern Welsh shows some interesting overlaps between the word for wisdom and trees:

gwydd   = trees
gwyddon   = magician
gwyddor   = rudiment, science, *Yr Wyddor* = alphabet

Fig. 5:1   Aradach Fionn: Fionn's Ladder

Table 5:2   A List of Oghams

Letter	Bird	Colour	Fortress
B	besan pheasant	bán white	Bruden
L	lachu duck	liath grey	Liffey
F	faelinn gull	flann red	Femen
S	seg hawk	sodath comely	Seolae
N	naescu snipe	necht clear	Nephin
H	hadaig raven	huath terrible	h-Ocha
D	droen wren	dub black	Dinn Ríg
T	triuth starling	temen dark grey	Tara
C		cron brown	Cera
Q	querc hen	quiar mouse	Corainn
M	mintan titmouse	mbracht variegated	Meath
G	géis swan	gorm blue	Gabur
NG	ngeigh goose	nglas green	nGarman
STR	stmólach thrush	sorcha bright	Strealae
R	rócnat rook	ruadh red	Roigne
A	aidhircleóg lapwing	alad piebald	Cualand
O	odoroscrach scrat	odhar dun	Odba
U	uiseóg lark	usgdha resinous	Usney
E	ela swan	erc red	Navan
I	illait eagle	irfind very white	Islay

Significantly, Gwydion, the most showy magician of British tradition, derives his name from the same root – gwydd. He is prominent in the Battle of the Trees, in which shrubs and trees are changed into warriors. This gnomic poem, attributed to Taliesin, may be taken on many levels. It is probably a teaching device about the nature of poetry and wisdom.

The battle itself is said to have been caused thus:

Three Futile Battles of the Island of Britain
One of them was the Battle of Goddeu: it was brought about by the cause of the bitch, together with the roebuck and the plover.[31]

These are the englyns that were sung at the Cad Goddeu, or as others call it, the Battle of Achren (Trees), which was on account of a white roebuck, and a whelp; and they came from Annwn, and Amathaon ap Don brought them. And therefore,

Amathaon ap Don, and Arawn, King of Annwn, fought. And there was a man in that battle, who unless his name were known could not be overcome, and there was on the other side a woman called Achren, and unless her name were known her party could not be overcome. And Gwydion ap Don guessed the name of the man, and sang the two englyns following:

> Sure-footed is my steed impelled by the spur;
> The high sprigs of alder are on they shield;
> Bran art thou called, of the glittering branches.

> Sure-hoofed is my steed in the day of battle:
> The high sprigs of alder are in thy hand;
> Bran thou art, by the branch thou bearest –
> Amathaon the Good has prevailed.[53]

Robert Graves' exposition of this poem in *The White Goddess* has furnished the modern Celtic magical revival with much food for thought, including the institution of a Tree Calendar. Graves' Tree Calendar utilised the Ogham alphabet to designate one lunar month per tree – a system which has since been taken to many hearts, but which has no prior precedent in Celtic tradition. Doubtless, certain trees were prominently part of seasonal lore, as today, but there is no suggestion in tradition for assuming their use in a calendar. (See Exercises.)

The lure of arcane knowledge has tempted many into making wild claims for the tree alphabet. To set matters in proportion, we need to see ogham for what it is: a Celtic method of inscription which has its roots in the tree-lore of native belief. When a word beginning with b was spoken, it automatically resonated with the birch-tree, with its lore, symbolism and power.

The real battle of the trees was one of words, of letters. The real warriors in this battle were the poets who wielded their oghams skilfully and to such effect.

6•THE BLESSED OTHERWORLD

Perhaps more than any other people, the Celts have always cherished the country of their true home – the Otherworld. It is the source of their wisdom, the place of their gods, the dimension in which poets and wanderers are most at home. Whoever has visited the Otherworld becomes more than mortal.

The Otherworld is generally understood to lie close to the borders of the manifest world, but, more especially, to lie within the compass of one ship's sailing, to the islands of the furthest West. Many wonder-voyages are taken to reach those shores; these are so numerous in Irish tradition that they constitute a genre of storytelling – the *immrama*.

Drinking birds

The realms of the Otherworld are those of the ever-living, where everything is possible, where great deeds are accomplished. The texts speak of a life which is enhanced to perfection, not an impossible heaven; in the Otherworld, life goes on as in the manifest world, with eating and drinking, making love and merriment. So wonderful is the Otherworld that we find descriptions of it in both pagan and Christian stories, with scarcely any modification.

Descriptions of the Otherworld evoke the most eloquent and lyrical of Celtic writing. Here is Loegaire, Cuchullain's charioteer, attempting to describe the sight which greets him when he enters the hallowed realms:

At the door toward the west
On the side toward the setting sun,
There is a troop of grey horses with dappled manes
And another troop of horses, purple-brown

At the door towards the east
Are three trees of purple glass.
From their tops a flock of birds sing a sweetly drawn-out song
For the children who live in the royal stronghold.

At the entrance to the enclosure is a tree
From whose branches there comes beautiful and harmonious music.
It is a tree of silver, which the sun illuminates.
It glistens like gold.[6]

We have already seen how time is convoluted and even folded to encompass the conception of Oengus (Chapter 2). The Otherworld is not bounded by the same constraints of time and space that govern our own world. Frequently, we find that heroes return after a year to find their contemporaries dead for many years, like Bran mac Febal who returns from his *immram* to find that his name is the stuff of legend. When one of his men attempts to leap ashore, he becomes as dust with the weight of his years.[21]

Nera returns from the *sidhe* after what has been for him three days, to find no time has passed at all. He also finds that the *sidhe* mound he has entered contains a whole community, with houses and lands.[98]

GOD OF THE ISLANDED SEAS

If there is any deity who may stand as patron for the Blessed Isles, it is Manannan. Keating records that his proper name was Oirbsean,[62] adding mysteriously that 'after a hundred conflicts he died'. This seems to refer to the number of incarnations or exemplars Manannan has had, including Fionn and Mongan. (See Chapter 7.)

One of Manannan's chief dwellings is said to be Emain Abhlach or the Isle of Arran off the west coast of Scotland. This has been identified as a prototype of Avalon.

Both Manannan and his British counterpart, Manawyddan, have the reputation of being 'night-visiting' gods. Each comes to women at nighttime and begets heroes upon them.

It is Manannan who sends one of his women to entice Bran mac Febal to make his *immram* or wonder-voyage. Bran awakes to find a branch of the magical Otherworldly tree in his hand and listens to the woman's song:

> There is a distant isle,
> Around which sea-horses glisten:
> Let not your intoxication overcome thee;
> Begin a voyage across the clear sea,
> If perchance thou mayst reach the land of women.[6]

Nothing loath, Bran mac Febal follows her advice and meets with Manannan mac Lir himself, who tells Bran about the country of Tir fa Thonn, the Land Under Wave. He and company do reach the island of women and, despite many protestations to stay, Bran eventually leaves to find his own world again.

These *immrama* stories are numerous and virtually give us a Celtic 'Book of the Dead' in their descriptions of Otherworldly islands whose powers and effects are charted upon the spirits of the company who sail thither. As each ship sails further into the West, so it is drawn closer into the nature of the Otherworld itself. Drawing upon such stories, the *Voyage of St Brendan* tells of a similar voyage undergone by the saint to find the Land of Promise. After many years' wandering and adventures, including the saying of Mass upon a whale's back, Brendan reaches his goal, but he turns back, returning to his own time and place once more.[54]

Tir fa Thon or Land Under Wave is not only an Irish phenomenon, since Taliesin refers to it also:

> There are three springs
> Under the mountain of gifts.
> There is a citadel
> Under the wave of the ocean[78]

One such stream has become the Celtic byword for wisdom.

THE SOURCE OF WISDOM

The Otherworldly well of wisdom, called the Well of Segais or Conla's Well, is the ultimate source of wisdom in Irish mythology. It is also the source of the River Boyne, so called after the goddess, Boann. According to the *Dindsenchas*, she went to test the well's power, and challenged it by walking three times widdershins about it. Three waves from the well rose up and drowned her.[6]

When King Cormac goes to the Otherworldly palace of Manannan, he discovers

> . . . a shining fountain, with five streams flowing out of it, and the hosts in turn drinking its water. Nine hazels of Buan grew over the well. The purple hazels dropped their nuts into the fountain, and five salmon which were in the fountain severed them and sent their husks floating down the streams.

Manannan explains this vision:

> The fountain which thou sawest, with the five streams are the five senses through which knowledge is obtained. And no one will have knowledge who drinks not a draught out of the fountain itself and out of the streams. The folk of many arts are those who drink of them both.[6]

The 'folk of many arts' are of course the *aos dána*, poetkind.

The Boyne held a mystic place among Irish poets, and they often used images derived from this mythos to describe their craft. In 'The Colloquy of the Two Sages', the venerable poet Ferchertne is asked by the young poet Néde: 'Whence hast thou come?' Ferchertne replies:

> Along the elfmound of Nechtan's wife,
> along the forearm of Nuadu's wife,
> along the land of the sun,
> along the dwelling of the moon,
> along the young one's navel string.[28]

These references are to the myth of Boann, who lost a thigh, a forearm and an eye when the well overwhelmed her. 'The young one's navel string' refers to the god Oengus mac in Og, the son of Boann. And here we come into the main arena of the myth, for it is the juxtaposition of great wisdom with extreme youth that is the supreme feature of two important narratives: that of Fionn mac Cumhail's eating the salmon of wisdom, and of Taliesin's imbibing of the cauldron.

After Fionn had left his female fosterers, he encountered a woman mourning the death of her son. He had been slain by Liath Luachra, the very man who had struck the first wound on Fionn's father. Fionn ambushed Liath and slew him, at the same time recovering from him the crane-bag which Liath had stolen from Fionn's father. Because of this act 'he dared not to remain in Ireland unless he undertook poetry, for fear of the sons of Uirghriu and the sons of Morna.'[90]

This refers to the indemnity enjoyed by poets, whose honour-price was so high that few men would injure or kill a poet knowingly.

Fionn thus went to learn poetry from Finneces, who lived on the shores of the Boyne. At this point, he still bore his boyhood name, Deimne. Finneces (White-Wisdom) had been seeking for the salmon of wisdom for seven years, since it had been prophesied that he would find it, eat it and know everything. However, when it was found, Finneces entrusted its cooking to Deimne, who, though cautioned to eat nothing of the fish, nevertheless thrust his burnt thumb into his mouth where it had been splashed by the salmon's liquor. So it was the boy, not Finneces, who received the wisdom of the salmon. The old poet immediately recognised the boy as Fionn (The Fair One), naming him as the prophesied receiver of wisdom. In aftertimes, Fionn had only to put his thumb into his mouth to have prophetic knowledge.

Other versions of the story say that Fionn's thumb was trapped in the door of a *sidhe* mound and it was thus that he acquired his wisdom. Both accounts go to show how Fionn, ostensibly a warrior, became known for his great wisdom and poetry.[90]

This story is paralleled in the British story of Taliesin who, as the boy Gwion, was set to tend the cauldron in which Ceridwen was brewing a draught of wisdom to compensate her son Afagddu for his ugliness. A splash of the liquor landed on Gwion's finger and he thrust his finger into his mouth to cool it. He immediately knew everything, but Ceridwen was not as forbearing as Finneces. She chased Gwion through many transformations until he became a grain of wheat and she a red hen who swallowed him up. She subsequently gave birth to him and cast him forth on the waters in a leather bag. He was found by Elphin in the salmon-weir of his father, Gwyddno Garanhir (The Wood-Wise One, the Tall Crane) and named Taliesin (Radiant Brow), and, though only a baby, was a capable poet who vanquished all Elphin's enemies.[17,78]

Significantly, Taliesin confounds the bards of Maelgwn Gwynedd by making them play 'blerm blerm' on their lips with a finger, so that they sound idiotic or childish. This gesture, so reminiscent of Gwion's wisdom-bestowing accident, and of Fionn's own knowledge-giving thumb, is the archetypal gesture of the child.

Bound up in both myths, we find the common elements of extreme youth and great wisdom; the sucked finger or thumb; a being of great wisdom who seeks to become even wiser, but who is destined to fail; and the refutation of malice.

Although Fionn's story does not directly link him with Boann, the goddess of the Boyne, she is none the less present in the salmon which is consumed, while Taliesin is directly pursued by Ceridwen, whom he serves, eaten by her and born of her womb. The way in which he is cast upon the waters of the river to land in a salmon-weir cannot be symbolically accidental. Both Boann and Ceridwen are preservers of wisdom, goddesses of the source of knowledge. The only difference between them is that in Boann's myth, the more ancient of the two, she has *become* the life-bearing waters, while Ceridwen is still an active deity in her own right. Both goddesses are patrons of poetry who are frequently invoked.

The way in which both men exercise their abilities varies, since Fionn's knowledge is dependent upon his putting his thumb into his mouth. Taliesin is shown to be universally omniscient. However, it seems clear that both Fionn and Taliesin correspond to the archetype of Oengus or Mabon, the Young God, whose youth and wisdom totally overset the ingrained cunning or venerable knowledge of either ancestral gods or sage druids. They are both capable in the combat of knowledge since they have imbibed from its very source. This youthful ability to confound wise-men was later celebrated in the Celtic Church in the episode where Christ disputes with the elders of the Temple.

THE WAYS BETWEEN THE WORLDS

Within Celtic topography, certain sites have ever been understood to be the place of entry into the Otherworld. Very often the mound is a place of entry into the Otherworld, or a natural boundary where both worlds meet. Etain says that she will meet Ailill on the mound above his house, but it is Midir she meets while Ailill is cast into a magical sleep. Three times she tries to meet Ailill, but each time Midir, who is of the Otherworld, prevents him and takes his place.[8]

This meeting is very like that in the *Mabinogion* where Pwyll meets Rhiannon when he goes to the mound of Arberth to see what wonders will happen there.[17]

Sometimes there are a variety of ways to reach the worlds within, as in 'The Wasting Sickness of Cuchulainn', where Loegaire, Cuchullain's charioteer, goes to investigate the *sidhe*: 'They saw a bronze boat crossing the lake and coming towards them. They entered the boat and crossed to the island; there, they found a doorway, and a man appeared.'[8]

There are also certain bridges between the worlds. Bran the Blessed forms himself into one such between the lands of Britain and the Otherworld, represented as Ireland.[17] Maelduin crosses a crystal bridge to reach the Island of Women.[6]

Many gifts pass between mortals and the Otherworld folk. Froech is gifted with red-eared white cattle,[8] while Pwyll receives pigs from the Lord of the Underworld.[17] Often the gifts are Otherworldly abilities, like the gift of healing – given to one Welsh family – or the power to sing, make music or create poetry.

Most frequently, it is the faery mounds, the *sidhes*, which are the designated homes of Otherworldly beings. These are well-known in every Celtic country and carefully avoided by those who fear the power of the Otherworld. The lore of the *sidhe* has subsequently degenerated into faery superstition in many countries, but still milk is left out and only good words are used to describe the lepra folk, the brownies, the People of Peace, the corrigans – any number of beings who populate the boundaries of the Otherworld with ours.

THE WOMEN OF THE SIDHE

The innerworld of the *sidhe* is famous for its women, known as *bean-sidhe*, or banshees, as they become in later tradition. These women are described always as royally attired and full of magical power.

The women of the *sidhe* have passed into tradition as banshees, but this tradition has its roots in the old stories. The faery women who approach Froech are dressed in green headdresses with scarlet mantles and with silver animal bracelets on their arms. They are the women of his mother and of Boand. They come weeping and lamenting to the place where Froech stands near to death. They bear him away to heal him, but such is their lamentation that many people are overcome: 'thus it is that the musicians of Eriu possess the weeping of the women of the Síde.'[8]

Usually the *bean-sidhes* attempt to detain their visitants, for they are aware that much time has passed and that mortals will find their own world no more. In 'The Voyage of Maelduine' the Queen of the

Island of Women throws a sticky thread to secure Maelduine's boat, but his men cut the magical clew and sail back.[14]

These women appear as the tutelary guardians of Otherworldly lore and, like the sisterhoods mentioned in Chapter 1, frequently appear in bands of three or nine. We have already seen how frequently the *immramas* speak about the Island of Women, and this may be some indication of the strength of an Otherworldly tradition concerning native priesthoods of women.

The priestesses who lived on the isle of Sein, referred to by Pomponius Mela, may be related to their insular sisters, although they may equally be a grove of druidesses, able to unleash the winds and storms, being oracular and predictive, difficult to consult save by those who have come great distances to find them.[71]

In later tradition, such women become witches or supernatural beings who wail for the dead. Significantly, some families are said to have their own *bansidhe*, who bewails the impending death of one of its members. Such traditions betoken a close association of that family with the Otherworld.

The deathless ones of the Sidhe are not always women; sometimes men lend their aid in a struggle of arms, as they do in 'The Destruction of Da Derga's Hostel', where the nine pipers of Sidhe Brega accompany Conaire: 'Combat with them is combat with a shadow. They will slay and will not be slain.'[8]

MUSIC OF THE SIDHE

The power of music has ever belonged to the Otherworld. Even today, Celtic folklore is full of stories about musicians carried off by the fairies to satisfy this desire for music.

The Dagda's harper, Uaitne, was carried off by the Fomorians and Lugh, Ogma and the Dagda discovered the harp in the hall of Bres. Because the Dagda had bound melodies into the instrument so that they sounded only when he called, he sang out:

> Come *Daurdabla!* (Oak of Two Woods)
> Come *Coir-cethair-chuir!* (Four-angled music)
> Come summer, Come winter!
> Mouths of harps and bags and pipes.[6]

And the harp was impelled from the wall and killed nine men before it came to the Dagda's hand. Then, with the skill of *sidhe* in his fingers, he played the three strains by which harpers are renowned:

the wail-strain, by which the company fell to lamentation, the smile-strain, by which they rejoiced, and the sleep-strain, at which they slept, so enabling the gods to rescue the harper and escape unseen.

Oengus Og himself was visited by a dream-woman or *aisling* whose visits left him dispirited because he could not find where she had gone. He became ill and could not eat for desire of her love. The next night she returned, playing upon a *timpan* (a kind of psaltery), and sent him into sleep with her music. Eventually Oengus finds her and they fly across the Bruig in the form of two white birds, singing such music that all who hear them fall into a deep sleep for three days and nights.[55]

This quality of sleep-inducing music also belongs to the Birds of Rhiannon who bring the listener into the Otherworldly dimension by creating communion with their song. After the beheading of Bran the Blessed, they sing, causing the company to forget the hardships of battle and to lose all sense of time. The birds which Tadg meets in 'Echtra Thaidg mhéic Chéin' have similar as well as healing properties: 'There were white birds with purple heads and golden beaks. They sang with sweet harmony while eating the berries and their music was melodious and magnificent. They would bring sleep to sick people or those grievously wounded.'[64] To such music, Arthur listens in the Otherworldly regions of Avalon.[75]

Birds are particularly associated with the Otherworld or Otherworldly states. We have noted their use in divination. St Columba is adamant in his assertion:

> I adore not the voice of birds,
> Nor the *sreod*, nor a destiny on the earthly world,
> Nor a son, nor chance, nor woman:
> My *drui* is Christ the son of God.[51]

But music is a truthful language in which no falsehoods can be tolerated. It is so that we find in most Celtic Christian remains, the continuity of birdsong in paradise: 'Three score birds and five and three hundred, bright like snow, golden-winged, sing many songs from [the branches of the paradisal tree]; it is a right language they sing together, but the ears of men do not recognize it.'[54]

THE UNDERWORLD

Within the cosmology of the Celts lie older elements of native belief; prime among these is the Underworld. Due to accumulation of traditions, it is often hard to disentangle the Otherworld from the Underworld, yet the two traditions are distinct.

The Underworld was not conceived of as a hell or place of punishment, rather it is the primal, creative place where mortals and the gods of the Underworld enter into special relationships. Pwyll meets Arawn, King of Annwn, and becomes obliged to help him overcome an adversary. The two change places, Arawn becoming briefly the Lord of Dyfed, while Pwyll becomes Arawn and rules Annwn.[17] For his faithful service in Arawn's kingdom, Pwyll is given the title, Pen Annwn, or the head of the Underworld, and his family forever afterwards enjoys a special link with the Underworld.

One feature of the Underworld which reoccurs throughout Celtic tradition is the way in which the turning tower exemplifies the Underworld. 'Whatever part of the world CuRoi might be in, he sang a spell over his stronghold each night; it would then revolve as swiftly as a mill wheel turns, so that its entrance was never found after sunset.'[8] Cu Roi seems to be associated with the turning fortress of the Otherworld, since he captures Blanaid from a castle at whose door a magical wheel turns endlessly. This turning wheel is the mill in which the gods of the Underworld reside, in which the dead are remade, and initiates reborn.

A similar tower appears on Maelduine's *immram* when he sees the Island of the Mill; into its dark maw is fed everything which is begrudged in the world. It is tended by a great, ugly miller who turns its wheel.[54]

This description is echoed by the British poem, *Preiddeu Annwn*, in which Taliesin describes one of the *caers* of the Underworld as 'ever-turning'. This poem is particularly important in giving us a closer glimpse of the Underworld at first hand.

The chthonic power of the Underworld is never far away from the Celtic imagination, for while the blessed Otherworld may lie many days sailing to the west, beneath the very earth is an older, more primal place.

7•THE HERO'S GLORY

BIRTHS AND CONCEPTIONS

Throughout this chapter we will examine something of the world of the hero and heroine who inhabit the mythic structure of the old stories. Though they are not gods, they frequently follow the broad archetypal patterns of the gods. In an age which is very hung-up about gendural roles, it is refreshing to see that Celtic legend makes little distinction between the sexes when it comes to being at the heart of the action. Celtic women, on the whole, are not a stay-at-home crowd; they are provocative protagonists, able in both love and war, for these are inextricably twinned in Celtic myth, although it is perhaps only Deirdre who comes even close to the power of Helen to provoke the latter.

It is with the great heroes, Cuchulainn and Fionn mac Cumhail, that we are most familiar.[91,90] Both heroes are well represented in Irish tradition, having become national archetypes for heroism. In British tradition, only the Arthurian legends come anywhere near such popularity, the lesser heroes of Celtic times being quite absent from popular consciousness, though not from the texts.[75,72]

What is the archetypal pattern of the hero? The Celtic storytellers were so familiar with this pattern that they recognised different kinds of stories: births, conceptions, wooings, adventures, voyages, exiles, hostings, deaths, etc., in connection with certain heroes whose exploits were so various that the storyteller could keep one cycle going from Samhain to Beltain with no trouble.[95]

The criteria for any hero are that he or she should have a strange

Lur-playing warriors

conception and mysterious birth. Cuchulainn is credited with no less than three putative fathers: his physical father, Sualdaim; his foster-father, Conchobor mac Nessa; and his spiritual father, the god Lugh. This unique triple conception story represents many levels of the Cuchulainn mythos and testifies to the semi-immortal status conferred on heroes.[95]

Heroes do not have an easy time of it and are often fated with terrible *geasa* before birth, like Condla, whose father, Cuchulainn, gives Aoife a ring to give to their son and to send him to his father. But he lays a tragic set of *geasa* upon the unborn boy: not to turn aside for anyone, not to identify himself to anyone and never to refuse a fight. When Condla comes to Ireland, he is challenged by the best heroes of Ulster, and refuses to say who he is; so well does he fight that Cuchulainn is sent to overcome him, which he does. He then realises who the boy really is, but all too late.[6] The overcoming of the son by the father is a motif which we find again in the story of Lancelot and Galahad, within the Grail legends.[74]

The naming of the hero is a magical act, since to determine a proper name one has either to be a druid or else present at some prodigious childhood act of the hero which provokes the giving of a name.

Deirdruí is named by Cathbadh, who practises a form of divination by laying his hand on her mother's womb before the girl's birth. He correctly prophesies her sex, her name and her deeds.[6]

The arming and naming of Llew Llaw Gyffes in 'Math, Son of Mathonwy' presents unusual difficulty since his mother, Arianrhod, refuses to give him either, which, according to British custom she was obliged to do.[17] This amounts to a blunt refusal to acknowledge him as her son – an interesting insight into the matrilinear traditions of Celtic society in which a mother gave arms and a name to her child. After Rhiannon's lost child has been restored to her, she declares: 'At last my trouble is over.' The company declare that as it is right for a mother to name her child, so her long-lost son shall be called Pryderi from *pryder* or anxiety.[17]

THE PRODIGIOUS YOUTH

The Celtic hero is supernaturally prodigious. Size and age are no disability to him. The child, Pryderi, at the age of 2 was as large as a 6-year-old.[17] While Peredur, the Celtic Perceval, drives two deer home on foot, believing them to be goats without horns.[72]

In a macabre incident which could well be taken from any boy's fantasy comic, Cuchulainn's prowess is tested in an ordeal of manhood in which he discovers many phantoms on a field of battle where he has gone to find the wounded king. First of all he meets with a 'man with half a head bearing on his shoulders half a man'. The man asks to be relieved of his burden and when Cuchulainn refuses to help, the monster throws him down. 'Here is a poor apprentice-hero trampled under foot by a phantom,' mocks the voice of Badbh from a pile of corpses. Cuchulainn immediately arises at this, cuts off the monster's head and, with his hurley stick, propels the head before him like a ball all the way home![98]

Without doubt one of the most important features of the hero's career is his arming and naming. Cuchulainn receives his naming first, being called 'the Hound of Culainn' from his killing of the hound belonging to the smith Culainn. In recompense, the boy hero promises to act as Culainn's watchdog. He then gains his weapon by a series of sly feats of strength so that, discarding all other weapons as unworthy by breaking them, he receives the king's own weapons and chariot.[6]

The Celtic hero had a certain number of 'excellences and accomplishments, *buada* and *clessa* . . . as every Welsh hero has his *cynneddfau* or faculties'.[98] Cuchulainn has no less than nineteen *clessa*. Some of these included:

his gift of prudence until his warrior's flame appeared, the gift of feats, the gift of *buanfach* (a game like draughts), the gift of chess-playing, the gift of calculating, the gift of sooth-saying, the gift of discernment, the gift of beauty.[6]

Set against this were his defects: 'He was too young . . . too daring . . . and too beautiful.'[6] Which sums up the dilemma of the hero in one short sentence. Set against these excellences were his *geasa*, of course. Most of Cuchulainn's concern his guardianship of Ulster's borders, for his strength is Ulster's palladium. He is overcome by beings whose otherworldly knowledge helps them pierce his *geasa*. He is caught between his *geasa* when he is invited by the Daughters of Calatin to join their meal of a roasted dog. Now dog was taboo to him but then so was his refusal to join a meal. Caught between his *geasa*, he is overcome.

THE WOMEN WARRIORS

In Irish society both girls and boys were sent out of the families to be fostered in the household of a neighbouring tribe or individual. In this way great bonds were forged between foster-parent and child, as well as between their families. This system kept the tribe cohesive in a society prone to feud and deeds of vengeance.

Young boys often received their warrior-training at the hands of a woman-warrior rather than from a tribal champion. Women warriors were a common feature of Celtic society, though use of arms was not enforced on all women. It was St Adamnan who, in the sixth century, legislated against the necessity of women to fight as warriors in battle – up till that time a legal requirement of landed women.[61] The position of the woman warrior was one of teacher.

After the hero's arming and naming, follows his initiation into sexuality, which is undertaken by skilled women. There are aspects of a dual course of weapon-training and love in Cuchulainn's trip to Alba to learn of Scathach. Scathach, the eponymous goddess of the Isle of Skye, is perhaps the most famous woman warrior. To her island centre are drawn many boys, each of whom has to cross a swaying bridge which repels all comers. Cuchulainn makes the hero's 'salmon-leap' and lands safely in her territory. During this period, Scathach teaches him her deadliest arts, while her prophetic daughter, Uathach, sleeps with Cuchulainn teaching him about love.[6]

In after-years, Cuchulainn's battle-frenzy is only prevented by the women of the tribe going out before the fort and bearing their breasts or appearing naked. Sjoestedt has questioned whether this might be analogous to the action of the Gaulish women of Gergovia who bared their breasts to the Roman troops in hopes of mercy. (Caesar's *The Gallic Wars*, VII, 47.) There is likely to be a sacred reason implicit in this action, with the women of the tribe acting as peace-makers.[98]

Some women became warriors out of necessity. Creidne had three sons by her father, the king of Ireland. Fearing his queen's displeasure, he banished his incestuously conceived children so that Creidne, in revenge, brought together three companies of *fianna* with whom she herself fought. She fought on sea as well as on land and wore her hair in braids. That is why men called her Creidne the Fèinid.' She fought thus for seven years until making peace with her father.[62]

The woman warrior stems from the mythological archetype of the Morrighan, implacable in battle, relentless in pursuit. Cuchulainn's career is dogged by the Morrighan and her sisters. In 'The Cattle Raid of Regamna', he meets Badbh as a red woman on a strangely yoked chariot. It is led by a red horse with one leg, with the chariot-pole through its body. He has a riddling dialogue with its occupant – a red-haired woman, cloaked in red – and eventually challenges her. But as he leaps into the chariot, only a crow remains – Badbh herself.[64] This triple-aspected warrior goddess never leaves Cuchulainn and, at his death, tied to the pillar stone where he had strapped himself in order to prolong combat, the Morrighan comes and sits on his shoulder.[6] The statue of this scene adorns the Post Office in Dublin where some of the bloodiest fighting was sustained during the Irish Civil War.

TWO DEADLY PANGS

In 'The Wooing of Etain', King Ailill is gravely ill. A doctor is brought to him and makes this diagnosis: 'You have one of two deadly pangs that no doctor can cure: the pang of love and the pang of jealousy.'[8]

It is so that Cuchulainn and Emer suffer: he for love of Fand, an Otherworldly woman, and she for jealousy of his love. As Emer remarks to her husband: 'What's red is beautiful, what's new is bright, what's tall is fair, what's familiar is stale. The unknown is honoured, the known is neglected – until all is known. Lad, we lived together in harmony once, and we could do so again if only I still pleased you.'[8]

Love strikes suddenly and without warning. The unfortunate

Deirdruí is enclaustrated from the sight of young men that she might never provoke the strife which is predicted by Cathbad the druid. But even in this place she experiences the pangs of love. She sees her foster-father flaying a calf in the snow:

> And the blood of the calf lay upon the snow, and she saw a black raven which came down to drink it. 'Leborcham,' said Deirdruí, 'that man only will I love, who hath the three colours that I see yonder, – his hair as black as the raven, his cheeks red like the blood, and his body as white as the snow.'
>
> 'Blessing and good fortune to thee! said Leborcham, 'that man is not far away. He is yonder in the stronghold of Emain Macha, which is nigh; and the name of him is Naisi, the son of Usnech.'[6]

And so begins the tragic story of Deirdruí and Naoisi.

As with Deirdruí's vision, Cuchulainn cannot be disturbed from his vision of the *bean-sidhe*. He lies catatonic, in a trance, while his charioteer, Loegaire, visits the Otherworld to bring the healing love of Fand. But it is not an affair which prospers anyone. At the last, Emer is forced to bring in the druids of Ulster to bind the lovesick Cuchulainn with spells and incantations: 'Then the druids gave him a drink of forgetfulness, so that afterwards he had no more remembrance of Fand nor of anything else that he had then done; and they also gave a drink of forgetfulness to Emer that she might forget her jealousy.'[8]

In British tradition, it is Lleu Llaw Gyffes who is overcome by his own loving trust. Cursed by his mother with a *geasa* which forbids him marrying with any mortal woman, Lleu's uncles, Gwydion and Math, form one out of flowers for him. Blodeuwedd is never asked whether she loves Lleu, but is conjured out of the Otherworld for his use. She immediately falls in love with Gronw Pebr and, with him, plots Lleu's death. Feigning anxiety about this event, she draws from him the circumstances which will accomplish it. Lleu tells her:

> 'I cannot be slain within a house, nor without . . . [neither] on horseback nor on foot . . .' 'In what manner then canst thou be slain?' 'By making a bath for me by the side of a river, and by putting a roof over the cauldron, and thatching it well and tightly, and bringing a buck, and putting it beside the cauldron. Then if I place one foot on the buck's back and the other on the edge of the cauldron, whoever strikes me thus will cause my death.'[17]

One last *geasa* is overcome by Gronw Pebr: he makes the spear to kill Lleu, which must be forged only during the saying of mass over the course of a year. Blodeuwedd inveigles Lleu to act out this deathly scenario in order to allay her supposed fears and so Lleu is slain.

But it is perhaps the fate of Deirdruí that sticks in mind most. Fated before birth to be none other than the wife of Conchobor, the King of Ulster; raised in seclusion, she falls in love with Naosi and suffers exile with him in order for them to be together. When, at the last, they are lured back to Ireland with the promise of indemnity, Naoisi is summarily slain and Deirdruí is brought before Conchobor and Eogan, the murderer of Naoisi. Conchobor determines that she shall live one year with him and one with Eogan. He says:

> 'Ha, Deirduí . . . it is the same glance that a ewe gives when between two rams that thou sharest now between me and Eogan.' Now there was a great rock of stone in front of them, and Deirdruí struck her head upon that stone, and she shattered her head, and so she died.[6]

MONGAN

One of the most magical and little-known heroes of Celtic tradition is Mongan. His quick-wittedness and use of magic come as a welcome change from the often stereotyped Celtic hero, all whirling arms and gnashing teeth.

The conception of Mongan is wrought by magic. His father, Fiachna the White, King of Ulster, went to Scotland to aid his friend King Aedan in battle against the Saxons, leaving his wife at home. During his absence, she was visited by a noble-looking stranger who told her that Fiachna would surely die at the enemy's hand unless she lay with the stranger. 'If we . . . make love, thou wilt bear a son thereof [who will] be famous.' The stranger likewise said that he would go to Scotland and avert Fiachna's death by fighting his assailant. When the stranger left her in the morning, he sang this quatrain:

> I go home.
> The pale pure morning draws near:
> Manannan mac Ler
> Is the name of him who came to thee.[21]

On the same night of Mongan's birth was also born Dubh-Lacha (Black Duck) and both sets of parents agreed their son and daughter should be handfast. When Mongan was three nights old, Manannan came for him and took him to the Land of Promise where he was to learn the Otherworldly arts of his father. Manannan promised to return him before he was 12 years old.

After his marriage to Dubh-Lacha, Mongan was visiting the King of Leinster when he was enchanted with a herd of fifty white red-eared cattle. He wanted them more than anything, and the King of Leinster, seeing his desire, remarked that they were a match for Dubh-Lacha. Mongan absent-mindedly agreed. He returned home with the cattle, shortly followed by the King of Leinster. 'I will give you anything in the province of Ulster,' Mongan promised. The King of Leinster demanded Dubh-Lacha for his own wife and Mongan had to let her go, because he had given his word.

The resourceful Dubh-Lacha made her abductor promise not to touch her for a year. She took with her her maid, who was Mac an Daimh's wife. Mongan fell into a decline until roused by his servant Mac an Daimh, also without his wife, accused him of learning nothing profitable in the Land of Promise. Mongan immediately fell to action and bade his servant fetch a shoulder bag and two sods of earth which came from Ireland and Scotland respectively. He would travel on Mac an Daimh's back with the sods underneath him, therefore making the King of Leinster's druids think that Mongan had one foot in Ireland and the other in Scotland.

On the way they passed a cleric, Tibraide, and his servant. Mongan magically created a partial bridge over which the cleric passed and fell into the river. Mongan seized his gospel book and took on the shape of Tibraide, while Mac an Daimh took the likeness of his servant. Having read the gospels to the King while Mac an Daimh loudly proclaimed 'amen, amen', Mongan proceeded to where Dubh-Lacha was in order to hear her confession. As soon as they were both within, Mongan and Mac an Daimh seized their own wives and jumped into bed with them.

Meanwhile, outside, the real Tibraide had arrived at court. Everyone declared they had never seen such a year for plentiful Tibraides! Tumbling to his ruse, the King of Leinster attacked, and Mongan and his servant were forced to retreat. Twice more, Mongan attempted to rescue Dubh-Lacha, swearing that no man should die on his account, since it was by his own folly that he had lost his wife.

Finally, Mongan asked the help of Cuimne, the Hag of the Mill. She was enchanted by his magic wand into a lovely woman, Ibhell of the Shining Cheek, daughter of the King of Munster, while Mongan himself took the shape of Aed the Beautiful, son of the King of

Connacht. Together they visited the King of Leinster, who fell hopelessly in love with the enchanted hag. Mongan was able to strike a bargain with the King – the hag for Dubh-Lacha, and together they made good their escape. In the morning, the King of Leinster found himself in bed with the Hag of the Mill, to his eternal shame.

This humorous story shares common elements with the story of Pwyll and Rhiannon,[17] where otherworldly animals are given as gifts and where the hero inadvertently gives up his wife to another. Mongan wins Dubh-Lacha back by guile and magic rather than by force of arms, yet, despite the humorous stories attached to him, Mongan has more mysterious components to his character.

A curious little tradition about him relates how Mongan and Fionn mac Cumhail were believed to be the same person. Mongan's overbearing poet, Forgoll, held that the warrior Fothad Airgdech had been killed at Duffey in Leinster. Mongan hotly disputed this assertion, wherat Forgoll began to threaten a terrible satire on his patron. Mongan offered his poet all the riches in his power unless he could vindicate his claim within three days. Mongan's wife, Breothigernd, was distraught with grief, but Mongan had already mysteriously begun his vindication. He said to her: 'Woman, be not sorrowful. He who is even now coming to our help, I hear his feet in the Labrinne . . . I hear his feet in the Main . . . I hear his feet in the Morning-Star River.'

Forgoll was preparing to take possession of the sureties offered by Mongan when a mysterious stranger entered the fort, leaping over walls to stand by Mongan's side. The stranger had a headless spear-shaft in his hand and Mongan called on him to report the truth of the dispute.

The stranger began to say: 'We were with thee, with Fionn . . . until Mongan stopped him. The stranger continued: 'We met with Fothad Airgdech here yonder on the Larne river. . . . I made a cast at him which went through him and . . . into the earth, leaving its iron head in the earth. This here is the shaft that was in that spear. The bare stone from which I made that cast will be found and the iron head will be found in the earth, and the tomb of Fothad Airgdech will be found a little east of it. A stone chest is about him . . . upon the chest are his two bracelets of silver, and his two arm-rings, and his neck-torque of silver. And by his tomb is a stone pillar. And on the end of the pillar that is in the earth there is an Ogham: "This is Eochaid Airdech. Caílte slew me in an encounter against Fionn."'

And so it was that Mongan's assertion was vindicated and from this story, in which one of Fionn's heroes appears in Mongan's defence, is it presumed that Mongan had been the same as Fionn mac Cumhail.

But this is not the end of Mongan's seemingly endless appearances. In 'The Voyage of Bran mac Febal', Bran encounters Manannan mac Lir, who tells him of a great prophecy concerning the coming of Mongan:

> Manannan the descendant of Lir will be
> A vigorous bed-fellow to Caintigern:
> He shall be called to his son in the Beautiful world,
> Fiachna will acknowledge him as his son.
>
> He will delight the company of every fairy-knoll,
> He will be the darling of every goodly land,
> He will be a dragon before hosts at the onset,
> He will be a wolf of every great forest.
>
> He will be a stag with horns of silver,
> In the land where chariots are driven,
> He will be a speckled salmon in a full pool,
> He will be a seal, he will be a fair-white swan.
>
> He will be throughout long ages
> An hundred years in fair kingship,
> He will cut down battalions – a lasting grave –
> He will redden fields, a wheel around the tract . . .
>
> Manannan, the son of Lir,
> Will be his father, his tutor.
> He will be – his time will be short –
> Fifty years in this world:
> A dragonstone from the sea will kill him
> In the fight at Senlabor.
>
> He will ask a drink from Loch Lo,
> While he looks at the stream of blood,
> The White host will take him under a wheel of clouds,
> To the gathering where there is no sorrow.[21]

This moving prophecy of Mongan's brief life is bound up inextricably with the coming of Christ within this poem; the implication being that Mongan is a great exemplar of the Otherworld who is conceived by a god and yet suffers the fate of mortals. Indeed Mongan is representative of all heroes whose glory is briefly enjoyed, redounding to the honour of their tribe.

Like a pair of yoked swans, the heroes of Celtic legend – both male and female – transcend the earthly planes in search of greater glory. Theirs is a short struggle and an eternal name.

8·THE YEAR'S TURNING

THE CELTIC YEAR

The Celtic Year was divided by a mixture of solar and lunar festivals. The equal-armed cross of the solar divisions was offset by the St Andrew's Cross of the lunar fire-festivals, each of which was celebrated on the full-moon.

The solar solstices and equinoxes are the marker points for the sun's path: at its zenith on the Summer Solstice, at its apogee at the Winter Solstice and at the two median points at the equinoxes. The lunar festivals, frequently called 'Celtic fire-festivals' because of the nature of ritual which attended them, marked important points in the Celtic

Fig. 8:1   The Wheel of the Celtic Year

calendar. Of course, the calendrical dates given above represent the fixed dates on which these festivals are celebrated today. As we will see from the Coligny Calendar on p. 115, the lunations cannot be fixed on calendrical dating, but follow their own pattern. The lunar festivals are concerned with pastoral and agricultural events, rather than the movements of the sun through the seasons.

Samhain and Beltain were the two major festivals, since they marked the division of the year into two parts: Winter and Summer. This is reflected in the lives of all Celtic peoples. At Samhain, beasts were rounded up and brought into stockades for wintering over; excess livestock was slaughtered, since they could not be kept alive during the hard months of cold and dearth of grain. At Beltain, herds were driven out into summer pasture, for the last of the frosts were safely over and livestock could be fattened up without fear of wolves.

These festivals also regulated the exercise of war and raiding. The Fianna hunted and engaged in warfare from Beltain to Samhain, in the warm months, and from Samhain to Beltain lived off the country, being billeted in different households and tribes.[90]

Both festivals were considered to be the prime time to communicate with the Otherworld. The doors of the *sidhe* were thought to be open on these nights.

The Celtic New Year was celebrated at Samhain, now celebrated world-wide as All Hallows, Hallowe'en or All Saints Day. This festival ushered in the new year, and marked the beginning of winter. The cold time was considered to be under the aegis of the Cailleach and so the rituals of Samhain were concerned with the dead, with divination and storytelling. These customs survive in the modern festival of Hallowe'en, as well as more authentically in regional parts as 'Mischief Night' or 'Punky Night'. The Christian feast of All Souls on 2nd November has drawn upon many levels of these customs, but the Celtic festival of Samhain has undoubtedly influenced it most. Many Catholic people in Europe and the Americas go to cemeteries on this day and light candles on the graves of their dead. In Britain, this feature is retained a few days later on Remembrance Sunday or Armistice Day, 11th November, when the fallen of the two World Wars are honoured. The bonfires of Samhain are now more likely to be lit, in Britain, on 5th November where Guy Fawkes Night has taken over the sacrificial aspect of this feast.

The feast of Oimelc marked the loosening of Winter's grip. At this time, the new lambs were born and ewes were in milk. In an age which depends on the artificial production of foodstuffs by modern farming methods, it is hard to imagine what winter would have been like without fresh milk to hand. Yet neither ewes nor cows will lactate unless they have given birth. The protein from new milk, butter, cheese and whey, not to mention the pies made from the docked tails of lambs, would have often made the difference between life and death for the very old and the very young during the hard frosts of February. Little tribal celebration was observed at this dark time of year, but the women met together to celebrate the return of the maiden aspect of the Goddess at the time when the Cailleach's winter was beginning to retreat a little. The many customs surrounding Brigit's feast will be discussed below.

Beltain or May Eve marked the real beginning of summer, the time when leaves were beginning to show and when flowers made every meadow colourful. This was the first real opportunity for the tribe to leave its winter quarters and go visiting. An extended clan would be able to gather together to celebrate this feast, discuss the news and make plans for the coming season. It was at this time that major gatherings and fairs were held. Beasts were purified from their long winter confinement in barns and yards by being driven between two fires, so killing off any possible lingering infections. This feast was under the aegis of the Shining One, Belenos, though we lack much reference to the nature of his rites. The release from winter confinement heralded ecstatic celebrations. As the *sidhe* doors were open, this night was also one for the Faery revels. Irish law tracts cite Beltain as the time of divorce. As trial marriages were normally made at Lughnasadh, we can deduce that the couple had had the long duration and confinement of winter to try their relationship and Beltain must have offered the first real opportunity to come before a *brehon* and declare their relationship at an end.

Lughnasadh marked the gathering together of the tribe at high summer. The concerns of the hay harvest would be behind and the prospect of the wheat and barley harvest would be yet to reap. This was a time for showing off the speed of one's horses, of competing in contests of skill and strength; it was a time for arranging marriages also, since young people would be foremost in exhibiting their quality at this festival and would form natural attachments which their parents might, or might not, think suitable. Marriages could be either love-matches or arranged matches, with the interests of the clan at stake depending on the status of the youth or maiden. But it was at Lughnasadh that trial marriages were entered into. Thrusting their hands through a holed stone, the couple would promise to live together for a year and a day, and part after that time if they did not measure up to expectation. Though perhaps none of the maidens would have been quite as demanding as Emer, who in the wooing contest between her and Cuchulainn, says of her fortress: 'None comes to this plain who does not go without sleep from summer's end to the beginning of spring, from the beginning of spring to May-Day, and again from May-Day to the beginning of winter.'[6] In other words, from Lughnasadh to Oimelc, from Oimelc to Beltain, from Beltain to Samhain: in effect, her wooer must not slumber for a whole year!

MYTHS OF THE FESTIVALS

Attached to the different festivals are particular stories and traditions which reveal more to us about the nature of the Celtic year.

Samhain marked the beginning of winter and was thus under the influence of the Cailleach. After the plentiful autumn came the barren time, the time of Otherworldly spirits. As this was the night when the dead were considered to be in communion with the living, it was an unchancy time when few ventured outdoors.

This reluctance is neatly and sometimes humorously pointed up in 'The Adventures of Nera'. It was Samhain Eve and two captives had just been hanged on the gallows outside the rath of Ailill and Maeve of Connacht. Aillill offered a prize to anyone brave enough to go outside and put a withe around the foot of one of the corpses. Nera takes up the challenge and accomplishes the task. But as soon as he handles the body, Nera experiences all manner of adventures. He has a vision of the royal rath (hill-fort) of Cruachan burning and finds himself in the Otherworldly sidhe where he marries a beansidhe. She tells him that his vision has not yet happened and, giving him the fruits of summer to prove where he has been, she sends him back to his own time and place, making him promise to come for her and her child when Ailill comes to destroy the sidhe, as he surely will when he hears of the vision. All falls out as predicted, but Nera vanishes into the sidhe and is never seen again.[95] This story underlines the dangers of Samhain but is also typical of the kind of ghost story which people still delight in telling at midwinter.

There are many stories attached to this feast, including 'The Battle of Mag Tuiread', which is the great cosmic battle between the Tuatha de Danaan and the Fomorians.[6] 'The Intoxication of the Ulstermen' relates how the drunken company, led by Cuchulainn, wander wildly across Ireland during Samhain, confused by drink and darkness.[6] Stories of sacrifice are prominent, as we have seen from 'The Adventures of Nera' and the fate of the captives. The death of

Cuchulainn occurs at Samhain.[6] The death of the hero Muirchertach mac Erca is wrought by the *beansidhe* Sin (her name means 'storm'), whom Muirchertach marries. He is half-drowned in a vat and half-scorched in a burning house.[6]

There are fewer myths and stories about the feast of Oimelc. There is an obscure tradition which relates the origins of the feast of Samhain which has a direct bearing on our understanding of Oimelc. It comes in 'The Book of Lismore' and purports to explain why Samhain is also called the Feast of All Saints. The boys of Rome, says the story, traditionally played a game every year on this day. It was a board game with the figure of a hag at one end and the figure of a maiden at the other. The hag let loose a dragon against her opponent, while the maiden let loose a lamb. The lamb overcame the dragon. Then the hag sent a lion against the maiden, who caused a shower of hail which defeated it. Pope Boniface asked why the boys played this game and who had taught them. They replied that the Sibyl taught them, in token of Christ's combat with the devil. The pope then forbade the game, since Christ's coming was a historical fact.[72]

The explanation of this game might divert us from the real meaning. The hag is the Cailleach who stands at the edge of the season of Winter. Opposing her, at the other end, is the maiden, represented by Brigit. It is Brigit whose feast of Oimelc marks the failing of winter's strength, at which time lambs are born. The Cailleach is traditionally associated with rough weather, but here it is Brigit who sends rain. The transition of one season into another is aptly reflected in the mythos of Cailleach and Brigit. Throughout Celtic myth, cailleachs are transformed into beautiful maidens at crucial periods of transition. We have already seen how important this myth is to Celtic kingship rites (Chapter 3) with the transformation of the Goddess of Sovereignty. The Cailleach equally puts off her hideous appearance and transforms herself into the maiden aspect of Brigit once more at the festival of Oimelc.

The feast of Beltain may once have had stories about the Celtic deity, Belenos, attached to it, but these have not survived. Beltain contains the word *teine* or 'fire' within it and this is one of the main features of the ritual practised on this day. Keating records only that 'they used to offer sacrifice to the chief god they adored, who was called Beil.'[62] What does remain are the evidences of myth and folklore. The Gaelic tradition of going out on Easter Sunday or upon Whit Sunday to see the sun dancing may well have derived from the feast of Beltain, when, as today on May-morning, people rise early to fetch in the May at dawn. The manifestation of both Taliesin and

Pryderi occurs on May-Eve. Taliesin, reborn of Ceridwen's womb. is found by Elphin in a leather bag at the weir where he has gone to look for the spawning salmon.[17] Pryderi is found in the stable of Teyrnon, whose new-born colt is stolen every May-Eve and who resolves to see what entity keeps stealing it. He retains his colt, drives off the monstrous arm which attempts to snatch it, and simultaneously discovers Rhiannon's stolen child. In both instances, we observe that the Otherworld has been at work.

Beltain stands diametrically opposite the other major door of the year – Samhain – and the stories associated with this festival are nearly always about the enchantments of the Otherworld being overcome. Prime among these stories is that of Lludd and Llefelys (see p. 11). Significantly, Lludd is the son of Beli.[17,72]

Lughnasadh seems to have been primordially a feast of the Goddess of Sovereignty. Two stories relate how, after their testing, the kingly candidates should proceed to the fair of Tailtiu. Tailtiu was the queen of the Fir Bolg and the daughter of Mag Mor (Great Plain) and the fostermother of Lugh. She died of exhaustion after the labour of clearing the lands of Ireland for cultivation, and Lugh thereafter held a festival for her in commemoration.[98] This story is very like that of Macha, who likewise dies of exhaustion after a great feat.[98] Both stories seem to relate to the labours of the Goddess of the Land.

Similarly, myths concerning the captivity of the goddesses Carman and Tea are told. In every case, the feast of Lughnasadh is a commemoration of one of these goddesses at different locations. The myths suggest that a common festival was upheld, but that regional goddesses were honoured at this time.

This was a particularly important feast whose duration was for two weeks before and two weeks after the actual festival day. It is prophesied that, as long as the custom shall be maintained, so shall there be 'corn and milk in every house, peace and fine weather for the feast'.[98]

SACRED CENTRES

The notion that a country had its own sacred centre is common to the Celtic nations, as well as to others. These centres, however, are not always geographically central, but are mystical centres, dependent upon the older criteria of mythic tradition.

Britain has as its place of natural assembly, Salisbury Plain, with the great cursus and sacred burial mounds surrounding it. The age and uses of Stonehenge have been much disputed, but the fact that the blue stones were brought from the Presceli Mountains in Wales doubtless shows that an even earlier sacred centre was transplanted to Salisbury Plain by this action. Mythic tradition gives Oxford as Britain's ancient centre in the story of Lludd and Llefelys.[17] In Ireland, the plain of Tara fulfilled a similar function as assembly point and inauguration stone of kings.

The places in which the festivals were celebrated is most interesting. Keating records a, probably mythical and didactic, tradition about this in which the king, Tuathal, builds four fortresses in the four

Table 8:1   Location of Festival Sites

Fortress	Province	Festival	Method of Celebration
Tlachtgha	Munster	Samhain	Druids offer sacrifice to all the gods
Uisneach	Connacht	Beltain	Fair to exchange goods; worship of Bel; cattle driven between the two fires
Tailltiu	Ulster	Lughnasadh	Alliances of marriage and friendship made
Tara	Meath	Feast of Tara held every 3 years	Law-giving and record-keeping

provinces of Ireland (see Table 8:1). We note that Oimelc and the province of Leinster are omitted from this tradition. Oimelc, celebrated in February, is hardly the ideal time for assembly. The season of Samhain has its own in-gathering feeling, establishing the beginning of winter, the bringing in of cattle into barns and stockades, and a time of leisure such as we now experience briefly at Christmas. Keating is here recounting the major assemblies in one specific tradition, which is not to discard the idea that each festival would have had its own local celebration. The idea of Tara as the royal and sacred centre was probably a mythical rather than a political reality.[62]

The partition of Ireland into portions – from two, to four to five – is an interesting progression. In 'The Settling of the Manor of Tara' we hear how certain provinces of Ireland are renowned for certain qualities.[4] In Table 8:2 I have shown the festivals which might make up this mythic schema. Sacred time and sacred place are juxtaposed, making a sacred mandala of place, quality, direction and time.

Table 8:2   The Sacred Mandala of the Festivals

Quality	Direction	Province	Festival
Knowledge	West	Connacht	Beltain
War	North	Ulster	Lughnasadh
Prosperity	East	Leinster	Oimelc
Music	South	Munster	Samhain
Sovereignty	Centre	Tara	Feast of Tara

TRIBAL CELEBRATIONS

Each of the festivals was marked by a prohibition on violent behaviour, abduction, theft, the levying of debts, etc. There were severe penalties entailed for anyone contravening this custom, for such events ruptured the sacred communion of the tribe with the gods. Festivals occurred in holy time and behaviour should reflect that understanding.

Samhain was a feast of peace and friendship, during which no weapon was lifted. Midir advises Oengus to approach Elcmar on this day, since Elcmar will be carrying only a staff of white hazel, signifying peaceful intention.[8]

Although the distinctions between the *aos daoine* and other people were clear-cut, there did not exist the same distinction of 'priesthood' and 'laity' that we now have. All men and women were capable of mediating the gods, and everyone would have taken part in seasonal festivals. Within the limits of the festivals, people made their own fun, told stories and held contests. Men would have been prominent in the contests of strength, in horseracing, wrestling, hunting and fighting. It was Lugh who invented draughts, ballplay and horsemanship, according to tradition, and these sacred games are important in the celebration of the festivals.[28]

The year is marked by certain appropriate actions and these are apparent from a number of texts. We have the testimony of many stories that the major festivals included games and contests of skill, such as horseracing. The playing of board-games seems to have been associated with both Samhain and Beltain, as does the mythic beheading-game, although this is more closely allied to Midwinter in the later story of Gawain and the Green Knight.[77]

Women celebrated separate festivals rarely. The place of women in the festivals and celebrations of the tribe is not exactly known. The example of Oimelc is given below. But Pliny also writes: 'In Gaul there is a plant like the plantain, called *glastum*; with it the wives of the Britons, and their daughters-in-law, stain all the body, and at certain religious ceremonies march along naked, with a colour resembling that of Ethiopians.'[23] The plant he refers to is woad. What is interesting is that women *and their daughters-in-law* celebrate in this manner, suggesting that only married or sexually active women were permitted to adorn themselves in this way, possibly in honour of the Blue Hag, the Cailleach Bheur.

The rites of Brigit, celebrated at Oimelc have been transmitted to us via the regional customs of the Outer Hebrides. The women met together and made an image of the maiden aspect of the Goddess, dressed it in white and placed a crystal over its heart. Brigit was solemnly invited into the house by the female head of the household and many sacred songs and chants were sung. The character of this Hebridean celebration has the quality of a Celtic confinement: with the image of Brigit in a cradle-like basket and the familiar warmth of female companionship.[35]

THE COLIGNY CALENDAR

Despite the current popularity of Robert Graves' speculative Tree Calendar, there is no hard evidence to suggest that the Celts observed the year by dividing it into tree months.[53] The ogham inscriptions form an alphabet of trees, not a calendar. However, without doubt, different qualities, symbols, trees, animals and tasks were associated with different times of the year.

The only evidence we have for a Celtic calendar – a formal method of reckoning days – is the Gaulish Coligny Calendar which was discovered in 1897. It is dated to about the first century AD and consists of a mass of engraved bronze fragments which have been painstakingly put together and annotated. J. Monard, in his interesting survey, speculates that it was compiled by druids who wished to preserve the distinctive Celtic calendar at a time when the Julian Calendar was being introduced.[80] The Coligny Calendar was clearly the work of a team of dedicated observers, whose comments – *quite clear, cloudy, and semi-clear* – appear on the bronze tablets.

The Coligny Calendar reveals some significant features. It reckons the beginning of months from the full moon (which is easily seen on clear nights), rather than from the new moon which is more difficult to assess. It takes into account the intercalery days (the extra days which accumulate in any calendar which attempts to make orderly divisions of the year) by the addition of a thirteenth month. By this method, some years had twelve, others thirteen months. Each month was divided into two parts, suggesting that the normal period of reckoning was a fortnight and not a week. This is borne out in many traditional stories. The calendar shows that the Gaulish druids observed a thirty-year system made up of five cycles of 62 lunations and one cycle of 61 lunations.

In accordance with general Celtic custom, a new day is reckoned from sunset to sunset (a night and a day) rather than from our present horary reckoning by clock-time. This is reflected in the computation of festivals which start on the evening before, e.g. *Oidche Shamhain* – the eve of Samhain. It is possible that the Christian observance of festivals was influenced by Celtic monks used to working with this system.

The months were designated as shown in Table 8:3. (The meanings are from my translation, but the Gaulish originals are very obscure.)

Table 8:3   The Coligny Calendar

Month	Period	Meaning
Samonios	October/November	Seed-fall
Dumannios	November/December	The Darkest Depths
Riuros	December/January	Cold-time
Anagantios	January/February	Stay-home time (lit. 'unable to go out')
Ogronios	February/March	Time of Ice
Cutios	March/April	Time of Winds
Giamonios	April/May	Shoots-show
Simivisonios	May/June	Time of Brightness
Equos	June/July	Horse-time
Elembiuos	July/August	Claim-time
Edrinios	August/September	Arbitration-time
Cantlos	September/October	Song-time

The extra thirteenth lunation, was termed *Mid Samonios*, being duplicated. If we examine these months in connection with the restored calendar, we find that the lengths of months is variable, according to lunation cycles, so that days will fall the same in every year. For instance, 14 January 1989 is VIII Anaganti, but 14 January 1990 is IV Anaganti. This fluid method of time-keeping is not likely to have worried the Celts, who did not live by their personal organisers or filofax but by the cycles of the moon and the agricultural seasons.

The meanings of the months given above may appear unlikely, but they are borne out in Celtic and seasonal fact. Samonios, or Seed-Fall, refers to the falling nuts and seed-cases of autumn. November to April are aptly named for the season. While Giamonios, Shoots-Show, refers to the burgeoning seeds. Simivisonios, Time of Brightness, is when the sun is at its zenith and the air is particularly clear. Equos, Horse-Time, is the season suitable for travelling or visiting. Elembious is when the tribes gather together for Lughnasadh and the harvest fairs, where marriages are contracted and when cases are presented to the judges. Edrinios is the time of arbitration, when claims have been judged and a reckoning awarded. Cantlos is when poets end their circuit of the land and settle at a designated place for wintering in.

The Celtic year was then a complete and satisfying round, in which Otherworldly and real time overlapped.

9·THE PARADISE TREE

THE CELTIC CHURCH

Christ, the Word from the beginning, was from the beginning
our Teacher, and we never lost his teaching. Christianity was
in Asia a new thing: but there never was a time when the
Druids of Britain held not its doctrine.[40]

The transition between Celtic paganism and Celtic Christianity was
surprisingly easy. So easy, that the statement above may well bear
out the truth of the matter: that druidism and Christianity mutually
upheld common concepts.

What made Celtic Christianity different from Roman Christianity?
Much has been made of these very slight differences by nineteenth-
century Anglican scholars, anxious to prove that the Celtic Churches
were a kind of Anglican forerunner. Actual research among extant
texts reveals that the celebration of mass and the regulation of
religious life differed very little in its basic constituents. The differences arise from regional custom and usage.

Before the Synod of Whitby (664), the Celtic Churches upheld the
doctrines common to both Orthodoxy and Catholicism, of which the
Celtic Churches were a part. They upheld the divine and human
natures of Christ. They drew heavily on the Scriptures, especially the
books of Moses, for legal and spiritual precedents.

The missionary spirit possessed the Irish and British men and
women who embraced Christianity. Celtic missionaries were
responsible for Christianising as far north as Iceland and the Faroes,

Celtic cross

and as far south as Italy and Switzerland. Two forms of martyrdom were recognised: the red martyrdom of death under persecution; and the white martyrdom of exile, gladly embraced for the grace of preaching Christ to the pagan.[46]

Christian communities formed about these missionaries and around many religious individuals who were not officially in holy orders. In a manner reminiscent of the ancient Israelites, whose exploits were the daily reading of lettered Christians, these communities elected abbots as spiritual leaders – a role which was to become hereditary in some families, in true Celtic fashion.

Particular differences are discernible in the doctrine of Original Sin, which one prominent British churchman, Pelagius – born Morgan – denied. He held that each man was punishable for his own sins, not from any inherited guilt. A strain of Pelagianism has remained in the British character ever since.

The sabbath was frequently celebrated by Celtic Christians on Saturday – the original Jewish sabbath. 'The Second Life of St David' shows that the saint started his celebrations of the Lord's Day on Friday at sunset, for example.[69]

Communion was given under both kinds – both the bread and wine being offered to the faithful. Clerical celibacy, in common with the rest of the Christian world, was not yet enforced. Much has been recently made of the bishop's letter, addressed to two Breton priests, admonishing them for allowing women to distribute the chalice to the faithful at communion. These women are termed *conhospitae* and seem to have been a regional form of deaconess.[71] There is no further evidence of women's involvement in the administration of the sacraments, though many stories relating to St Brigit and other female saints show that women had a lot more latitude in the Celtic Church than was normally acceptable elsewhere.[16]

Perhaps the most telling difference between Celtic and Roman Christians was the Celtic manner of tonsure. The biased writings of Bede called this 'the tonsure of Simon Magus' in a slighting way. The Celtic clergy shaved their heads from ear to ear, sometimes leaving a tuft of hair in the centre. It is tempting to speculate whether this tonsure might have been inherited from the druids. The druid, Mog Ruith, has a whole series of stories in which he becomes the associate of Simon Magus, which might account for how Bede came by the name.[69]

The Synod of Whitby, called at the double monastery administered by St Hilda, to regularise the differences between the Celtic and Roman Churches, was most concerned about the Celtic method of dating Easter, which varied considerably from the Roman custom. St Colman and St Hilda supported the Celtic Church, but St Wilfrid opposed it. The ensuing decision by the British Church to follow the spiritual guidance of Rome rather than its Celtic missionaries from Ireland led to a grave division.

Monasticism was the Celtic Church's great mainstay – not the cloistered monasticism of the European Benedictine, but a kind similar to that still found in Egypt and Syria. Eremetical or coenobitic in character, the solitary monks of Skellig Michael off the south-west coast of Ireland typify the dedication and asceticism of the Celtic Church. The purity of such fierce asceticism was fanatically preserved by many individuals after the Synod of Whitby in 664. St Aldhelm, the Saxon abbot of Malmesbury and himself the pupil of a Celtic missionary, observed how the British priests beyond the Severn (i.e. Wales)

... have such a horror of communication with us that they refuse to pray with us in their churches, or to seat themselves at the same table ... what is left from our meals is thrown to the dogs and swine . . . and if one of us went to live in their country, the natives would not hold communications with him till after he had been made to endure a penance for forty days.[69]

Elements of this ascetic quality can still be discerned today in some of the Welsh Chapels, in Scottish Presbyterian churches and in many independent Christian sects of primitive persuasion.

The unique quality of Celtic spirituality did not suddenly cease. Elements of it survived locally in folk-customs and seasonal celebrations. Some of the most notable survivals were collected by Alexander Carmichael in the Hebrides. Those who want to sample the insights of the Celtic Church should consult his *Carmina Gadelica*, which is a veritable treasury of Celtic spirituality.[35]

THE GREAT KING'S SON

The identification of the Celtic soul with the sufferings and miracles of Christ is perhaps the key to the mystery of how Christianity found its way so readily into the heart of the Celtic peoples. Like the Anglo-Saxons, who found their identification with the young hero who strips himself to mount the tree in *The Dream of the Rood*, so too do the Celts identify themselves with the Passion of Christ in an intimate way. Just as St Clement of Alexandria wrote about Christ for the benefit of first-century Hellenic believers as a new Odysseus, bound to the mast of the great barque which is the Church, so too does the eighth-century Irish poet, Blathmac, write of Christ's crucifixion in the manner of a *fili* telling of the death of Cuchulainn:

> A fierce stream of blood boiled until the bark of every tree was red; there was blood throughout the world in the tops of every great wood.

> It would have been fitting for God's elements – the fair sea, the blue sky, the earth – to have changed their appearance, lamenting their calamity.[2]

Or here, with the dreadful power of ancient keening, we hear the authentic Celtic voice:

> At the cry of the first bird
> They began to crucify Thee,
> O cheek like a swan,
> It were not right ever to cease lamenting –

> It was like the parting of day from night.
> Ah! though sore the suffering
> Put upon the body of Mary's Son –
>
> Sorer to Him was the grief
> That was upon her for His sake.[19]

Consistently, the Celtic Christians write of the elemental chaos wrought by the crucifixion, particularly of the stopping of the sun. In 'The Settling of the Manor of Tara', we read how Trefuilgnid Treochar has left his place in the eastern margins of the world because the sun has risen in the west that day and he wants to know why.[4]

THE MASTER-STROKE OF WOMEN

This curious title, borrowed from the language of hurley, was given to Mary by the bardic poet, Pilib Bocht ó hUiginn. It expresses exactly just how the Celts revere Mary: a unique or, to borrow an Irishism, a smashing woman. In Irish, a special form of the name Mary is given to her: while little girls can be called Maíre, only the Mother of God can be called Muire.

The reverence which was shown to the many aspects of the Goddess in pagan Ireland has been partially bequeathed to the Blessed Virgin. The central place of the mother in Celtic society is borne out by an oral Hebridean saying:

> There is mother's heart in the heart of God.[2]

Which shows how non-dual the Celtic mind really is. Mary is greeted by all conditions of people with great wonder:

> What woman is like Mary, she the woman of the house to all?[70]

One of the bardic poets, Tadhg óg hUiginn, says of her:

> My relationship to her is closer than my nearest kindred.[70]

And it is this sense of family intimacy which transcends even that most ingrained of Celtic ties – the tribe – that makes Mary everyone's mother.

Mystically, Mary, like Danu or Don, is the nourishment of body and spirit:

> Chosen palace of the Almighty who bore the wheat that nourishes the race of Eve,[70]

as an oral Ulster poem on the life of Christ terms her. These are not extravagant phrases extrapolated from a pietistic cult, but vital leaves from the Celtic Tree of Life.

Not surprisingly, the triple Mother of Celtic tradition resurfaces in the many moving laments which surround the Crucifixion of Mac Mhuire or *Mab Mair* (Irish and Welsh for Mary's Son). Here, the keening of the Three Marys breaks out from the deepest sorrow of the world:

> Peter, Apostle, have you seen my love so bright?
> *M'ochón agus m'ochón ó*
> I saw him with his enemies – a harrowing sight!
> *M'ochón agus m'ochón ó.*
>
> Who is that fine man upon the Passion Tree?
> It is your Son, dear Mother, know you not me?
>
> Is that the wee babe I bore nine months in my womb?
> That was born in a stable when no house would give us room?
>
> Mother, be quiet, let not your heart be torn,
> My keening women, mother, are yet to be born! (Ní Riain)

Mary is universally invoked as a mother, yet she has also inherited the power of the Goddess, the Morrighan, as a protector:

> O vessel bearing the light, O great brightness outshining the sun, draw me ashore, under your protection, from the short-lived ship of the world. (Ní Riain)

This couplet, from a song known as 'The Breastplate of Mary', bears out the connections between the Morrighan (Great Queen or Sea-Queen) with Mary's special title *Muire* (Irish *muir* – sea). Just as the Great Goddess, Danu, Anu or Don was the mother of the Great Tribe which we have identified as the Celts, so Mary is the mother of a greater tribe, whose peoples are from every created race.

FOSTER MOTHER OF THE SON OF GOD

Just as the ancient Irish had difficulty in distinguishing between Danu, the Mother of the Gods, and Brigit, so too did the Christian Irish between Mary and St Brigit. Of all the saints in the Celtic world, it is St Brigit who has commanded most respect. This is perhaps not surprising, as we have seen that the Goddess of wisdom, poetic inspiration, smithcraft and agricultural fertility has occupied a central place in the Celtic heart as Mother. We have seen how many of the aspects of Anu, Danu and Don went into the making of Brigit and Brigantia. These same aspects filtered down into the mythos of St Brigit.

Bride, as she is familiarly called in Gaelic, occupies a unique place in Celtic Christianity, for apocryphal tradition places her strategically at the heart of the Incarnation as the 'foster-mother of the Great King's Son', of Christ himself.

A modern invocation to Bride shows how this respect and reverence still adheres to the ancient model (my translation):

> I take Bride as my advocate,
> Dear to me is Erin,
> Dear to me each land,
> Praise be to it!
>
> O white flame of Leinster,
> Enlighten the whole land,
> Chief of Erin's maidens,
> Chief of finest women.
>
> Dark the bitter winter,
> Cutting its sharpness;
> But Bride's mantle
> Brings spring to Ireland.[52]

This prayer refers to the eternal flame which burned in the sanctuary at Kildare. This holy fire was guarded by nineteen nuns who each took a turn to feed the flame. On the twentieth night, St Brigit herself took over. Only women were permitted to enter the enclosure where the fire burned and to blow up the fire with the bellows, never with the breath of their mouths, so Gerald of Wales records in his twelfth-century itinerary of Ireland.[11] The fire was not extinguished from the foundation of the monastery in the sixth century until the reign of Henry VIII, when the Reformation undid what centuries of devotion had preserved – a tradition whose roots undoubtedly spring from native Celtic belief. The devotion of the nuns of Kildare reminds us forcibly of the sisters of the Galliceniae, recorded by Posidonius, who jealously guarded their enclosure from intrusion by men, and whose rites were upheld through many generations.[71]

Also remembered here is the association between the festival of Oimelc and the Goddess Brigit. Just as the Goddess was concerned with the fertility of the land, so too is St Brigit associated with the new milk of sheep at lambing time. The late winter chill of February is softened by the bounty of sheep's milk.

The tradition of St Brigit as the fostermother of Christ is one of the major links between the pagan and Christian Celtic worlds. Many stories speak of how she was the aid-woman or midwife to Mary, and tell of how she helped Mary discover the lost child when he was left in the Temple by the aid of her divinatory skills.[35] Other stories tell of how St Brigit drew the attention of Herod's soldiers upon herself by acting as a fool, in order that Mary and her son could escape to Egypt.[39]

St Columba

Columba's birth was heralded by a prophecy:

> A manchild shall be born of his family,
> He will be a sage, a prophet, a poet,
> A lovable lamp, pure and clear.
>
> Who will not utter falsehood.
> He will be a sage, he will be pious,
> He will be King of the royal graces,
> He will be lasting, and will be ever good,
>
> He will be in the eternal Kingdom for his consolation.[40]

After his conception, his mother had a vision in which an angel handed her a beautiful mantle which spread out over the land. He was baptised Crimthan (Fox), becoming Columba (Dove) at his tonsuring. He was reputed to have Axal as his angel and Demal as his devil.

Of a royal family, Columba also had the benefit of a poetic education and was thus learned in both pagan and Christian traditions. He might be called the patron saint of photocopiers since he borrowed a book of psalms from Abbot Finnian of Moville and copied it secretly. When Finnian discovered the deception, he demanded the copy as well for 'to every cow belongeth her calf, to every book its little book'. This same book, the Cathach, has partially survived with its illuminated Celtic tracery and lively script.[51]

When Columba visited Longarad, a great poet, *seanchai* and judge, Longarad hid his books (possibly because of St Columba's reputation as a tardy returner of books?). Columba cursed him: 'May the cause of your miserliness be of little profit to you,' and shortly afterwards, Longarad died. This incident shows Columba as one who promoted the oral tradition and the dissemination of knowledge rather than keeping it hidden.

Columba's refractory nature caused him at one point to be scourged by an angel for refusing to ordain Aedhan as King. The angel appeared with 'the glassy book of the ordination of kings' in his hand and showed Columba what was written there, but Columba preferred Aedhan's brother, Iogenan, better. The mark of the scourge remained on his side until his death, a token of his disobedience.[1]

Columba, like many other Celtic saints, frequently enters into dispute with the druids. He has a magical battle with the Pictish druid, called 'a magus' of King Brude. He causes Briochan to be smitten with illness and then cures him by blessing a white stone which is put in Briochan's drink. Adamnan's life of Columba reveals that the saint was not beyond using druidic and poetic means to overcome his opponents.

As the founder of Iona and the patron of many Celtic missions, Columba's influence stretched wide across Britain.

LORICAS

The Celts, especially the Irish, developed a particular form of protective invocation or prayer known as a *lorica* (Irish *sciathlúireach*) or breastplate. So widespread is this notion in Celtic literature that we may assume that this form of protective spell originated with the pagan Celts or from the native peoples they assimilated.

St Patrick's breastplate is the most famous. It has gone into modern Christian tradition as the hymn, 'I bind unto myself today/The strong name of the Trinity.' In its original form, it displays great insight into the Celtic preoccupations with being enspelled and being protected by mighty powers, whether these be of God or of nature: indeed, the nature of the protection invokes the very elements themselves in a quite startling way:

> I arise today
> Through the strength of heaven:
> Light of sun,
> Radiance of moon,
> Splendour of fire,
> Speed of lightning,
> Swiftness of wind,
> Depth of sea,
> Stability of earth,
> Firmness of rock.[40]

The manner in which this invocation came about is interesting.

Patrick and his monks were in danger of being ambushed, so when he had to go out with eight of his young clerics and his servant, Benen, Patrick blessed them and 'a cloak of darkness went over them so that not a man of them appeared.' All that the pagan Irish saw were a troop of eight deer and a fawn with a white bird on its shoulder. And so Patrick uttered his lorica which is thereafter called 'The Deer's Cry'.

As we see, Patrick shares both the druidic ability to create invisibility and also to shapeshift. Significantly, he further asks to be protected from the spells of women, druids and smiths. This curious statement exactly shows where the native Irish invested their magical powers: the Otherworldly women of the *Sidhe*, the druids steeped in esoteric knowledge, and the wonder-working smiths, whose knowledge of metals put them into the magical class.

The following prayer, from an Irish medieval ms., gives the names of the archangels for each day of the week. As we have seen, the concept of particular days of the week belonging to or being under the protection of certain saints is widespread in Scots Gaelic:

> May Gabriel be with me on Sundays, and the power of the King of Heaven.
> May Gabriel be with me always that evil may not come to me nor injury.
>
> Michael on Monday I speak of, my mind is set on him,
> Not with anyone do I compare him but with Jesus, the son of Mary.
>
> If it be Tuesday, Raphael I mention, until the end comes, for my help.
> One of the seven whom I beseech, as long as I am on the field of the world.
>
> May Uriel be with me on Wednedsays, the abbot with high nobility.
> Against wound and against danger, against the sea of rough wind.
>
> Sariel on Thursday I speak of, against the swift waves of the sea,
> Against every evil that comes to a man, against every disease that seizes him.
>
> On the day of the second fast [Friday], Rumiel – a clear blessing – I have loved,

I say only the truth, good the friend I have taken.

May Panchel be with me on Saturdays, as long as I am on the yellow world.
.... [line missing from original] ....

May the Trinity protect me! may the Trinity defend me!
May the Trinity save me from every hurt, from every danger![32]

As we can see from the use of the angelic names, there is an extended understanding of apocryphal Christian sources which have not remained in Western Christian mysticism. Only Syrian and Coptic Orthodoxy have retained some of these angelic forms, which does lead us to the distinct possibility of a cross-fertilisation of Celtic Christianity by Middle Eastern Orthodoxy. Since the schism between the Western and Eastern Churches was not effected until 1054, and the Celtic Church was operational probably until a few years after the Synod of Whitby in 664, there was doubtless a good deal of communication between monks of both churches.

But the power of the lorica to protect has not departed, as we find from this Irish prayer, to be said before sleeping (my translation):

> God with me lying down, God with me sleeping.
> Evil be far from my sleeping and dreaming.
> The cross of Bride be under my feet,
> The mantle of Mary about my shoulders,
> The protection of Michael over me, taking my hand,
> And in my heart, the peace of the Son of Grace.
> If malice should threaten my life
> Then the Strong Son of God between me and evil.
> From tonight til a year from tonight,
>   And this very night,
>   And for ever,
>   And for eternity, Amen.[52]

SOUL-FRIENDS

The Celtic concept of soul-friend – a spiritual companion – is one which remains deep withn living tradition. In Celtic Christian tradition, the soul-friend was confidante and sometimes confessor. Modern Eastern Orthodoxy retains this same concept, whereby any holy lay man or woman can act as a soul-counsellor. Only unofficially does such a role obtain today.

The importance of soul-friends is shown in the life of St Comgall, who entered his church one day to find that it seemed to him that all present there were headless. He blessed the company with him so that they were also able to see what he saw. He told them: 'My soul-friend has died and I am without a head and you are without heads; for a man without a soul-friend is a body without a head.' Molua, his foster-son and student, bade someone lift up the gospels and pray before it till a new soul-friend was revealed, and so it was that Molua himself was chosen.[29]

The vindication of a soul-friend is given below. The verses, from the Life of St Moling, describe not only the perfect Christian, but the perfect hero – according to Celtic criteria:

> He is pure gold, he is a heaven round a sun,
> He is a vessel of silver with wine,
> He is an angel, he is wisdom of saints,
> Whoever doth the King's will . . .
>
> He is a sweet branch with its blossom,
> He is a vessel full of honey,
> He is a precious stone with its goodness,
> whoso doth the will of the Son of God of heaven . . .
>
> Whoso doth the will of the Son of God of heaven
> Is a brilliant sun round which is summer,
> Is an image of God of heaven,
> is a vessel glassen, pure.
>
> He is a race-horse over a smooth plain
> The man that strives for great God's kingdom,
> He is a chariot that is driven under a king,
> That bears off prizes in the east.
>
> He is a sun that warms holy heaven,
> A man for whom the great King is thankful:
> He is a temple prosperous, noble,
> He is a holy shrine which gold bedecks.
>
> He is an altar whereon wine is shed,
> Round which is sung a multitude of melodies;
> He is a cleansed chalice with liquor [therein],
> He is white-bronze, he is gold.[29]

With such images, it is easy to see how little the Celtic view of paradise differed from the pagan descriptions of the Otherworld.

10·THE ENDLESS KNOT

THE CHAIN OF LIFE

As we remarked in Chapter 1, the Celts have no creation myths as such. Their is a far more subtle series of interrelationships which transcend the need for a fixed end and beginning.

In *Cormac's Glossary* we come across this obscure gloss on the word *tuirgin*. It is described as:

> A birth that passes from every nature into another, i.e. a birth of the true nature . . . As Fachtna son of Senchaid says: 'he gives a transitory birth which has traversed all nature from Adam and goes through every wonderful time down to the world's doom. He gives the nature of one life . . . to the last person who shall be on the verge of judgement.[25]

This description could well be applied to many of the ancestral gods, heroes and poets whom we have met in this book: Tuan mac Carill, Mongan, Taliesin, Fintan, Etain, Ameirgin, Mabon, the Cailleach Beare and countless others. For these can all be said to change their lives in many ways, while giving continuous momentum to the endless Celtic know to existences.

It seem that the Celtic soul is deeply committed to this continuance

Book of Kells man with beast

of life. Through story, song, poetry, magical tradition, prophecy and augury, their insights into the deeper life are made clearer to us who are, to some extent, exiled of that tradition.

This chain of life is as far removed from the Buddhist principle of *samsara* – a continuous and weary round of incarnation which is conceived to have a welcome ending – as it is possible to find. The

Celtic chain of life is an endless knot of possibilities and varieties sustained and made possible by its firm roots in the primal traditions of myth and magic.

> A continuity of existence
> Still remained in me, which I do not deny[28]

says Fintan, who has lived from the time of Noah until the dissemination of Christianity as Ireland's 'true remembrancer'.

Mabon, the youngest and the oldest of the gods, bridges aeons of time in his own person and is only found by the expedient of consulting the most ancient animals of Britain.[73] To these ever-living beasts we now turn, to learn a deeper wisdom.

POWER OF THE TOTEMS

In a society where meat comes from a supermarket, milk from a bottle, fruit from a tin and bread from a packet, it is hard to conceive of the multi-dimensional nature of human dependency upon the animal and vegetable kingdoms. Yet this inter-species dependency was quite clear to the Celts. It was one of the open secrets of tradition, that the great chain of life stretched back beyond humanity to animals, birds, fish, trees and rocks long before modern theories of evolution were voiced. Such secrets were the *aos dána's* stock in trade: they derived their memory from a complexity of remembrances. Where human memory ran out, then the memory of animals, plants and rocks was available to be drawn upon.

Because the make-up of each person was individually different, each had access to a different set of memories, a different set of totems.

Totem is an Algonquian word now universally applied by anthropologists to define the hereditary emblem of a tribe, people or family. This emblem – usually an animal, but sometimes a tree or plant – is sometimes considered to be the ancestor of the tribe, a beast possessed of special wisdom which is shared by its descendants. But while we see examples of tribal totems in Celtic races, we frequently encounter people's individual totem: the guardian spirit whose life is contiguous with theirs.

Cuchulainn's fame is joined to his totem, the dog, which he is not allowed to eat: not only does he receive his naming from his struggle with the hound of Culainn the Smith, which he kills and in whose place he must be Culainn's watchdog, but his death is presaged by the saying that his first and last act would be the death of a dog. As he lies bleeding to death, an otter (water-dog) comes to lick his blood. He kills it with his sling.[6]

Throughout his life, he also shows his mastery of the inner world governed by the totems. He captures birds in flight and strings them to his chariot, as well as yoking a deer to pull his chariot. In his riddling wooing of Emer, he admits to having eaten of *the geasa of the chariot*, which Emer correctly identifies as horseflesh: the *geas* forbade anyone who had so eaten to step into a chariot for at least twenty-seven (three times nine) days.

Pryderi is stolen from Rhiannon's side and subsequently found by Teyrnon in a stable with a foal which becomes his companion.[17] Diarmuid O'Duibhne is forbidden to hunt any boar because his alter ego goes in that shape; it is so that he meets his end.[14]

Oisin is one example of inter-species mating. He is the son of Fionn and Sadbh, but was born to his mother when she was in deer-shape. He is destined to be in human shape if his mother does not lick him; however, unable to refrain from one act of tenderness, she gives him one such lick on the forehead where Oisin, which means 'little deer', retains a tuft of hair.[95]

POWER OF TRANSFORMATION

It is frequently said that the Celts believed in reincarnation. This is true, but the real picture is more complex. Let us define a few terms:

metamorphosis = a change of form
metempsychosis = a passing from one body to another after death
reincarnation = becoming born again

One of the most striking features of Celtic myth is the common ability for gods, poets and heroes to change shape. Perhaps the most illuminating story in this tradition is found in the story of Taliesin who, as Gwion Bach, undergoes the following transformations, pursued by Ceridwen:

Gwion	Ceridwen	Element
hare	greyhound	earth
fish	otter	water
bird	falcon	air
corn	hen	fire
Taliesin		

It will be seen that each level of transformation corresponds to one of the elements until Gwion becomes a grain of corn and is swallowed up by Ceridwen in hen's shape. He thereafter becomes a foetus in the womb of the Goddess and is reborn as Taliesin. Of course, this story can be taken on many levels. Such metamorphoses as this are firmly based in the Celtic initiatic mysteries of the bard into deeper knowledge and this story is clearly a Mystery narrative. This story combines metempsychosis, metamorphosis and reincarnation.[78]

Etain's transformations are really a metempsychosis, although they begin as a form of enchantment. Etain, the wife of Midir, foster-father of Oengus of the Bruig, was co-wife with Fuamnach, a druidess of great power. With her rowan wand, Fuamnach turns Etain successively into a pool of water, a worm, and a fly, but she is reborn of Etar as Etain again. This series of metempsychosis is said to be of one thousand and twelve years in duration. Having no memory of who she has been before, Etain marries Eochaid Airem, from whom Midir seeks to win his former wife by a series of *fidchell* contests. Eventually Midir carries Etain back to the Otherworld.[8]

It was said of Cuchulainn that his friends were anxious to get him married while young, since it was thought he would die young and leave no heir 'knowing that his rebirth would be of himself'.[6] However, he does not only die young, he also kills his only son, and his only continuance is his memory kept young in numerous stories.

As we have seen, the gods sometimes take on new or human shapes in order to enact the cosmic order. Manannan comes again in the shape of Fionn, it is said, and also as Mongan, though it is forbidden to mention this to him. (See Chapter 7.)

A SHAPESHIFTING STORY

The story of Math ap Mathonwy gives us the greatest combination of magical shapeshifting in Celtic tradition.[17] Math himself is the primary druid of the British tradition – his name means 'Bear, son of Bearlike', a clear imputation of the totem beast from whom he derives his power. The Celtic proverb, 'a bear for wisdom' is applicable to Math, whose own abilities have become proverbial in British tradition:

> There are few who know
> Where the magic wand of Mathowny
> Grows in the grove.[78]

The chief shapeshifter in the story is Gwydion. He raises war in order to distract Math and to leave Math's royal footholder, Goewin, vulnerable to the advances of Gwydion's brother, Gilfaethwy. In order to accomplish this war, he goes to demand the pigs of Pryderi of Dyfed, who got them from Annwn. By a spell he makes twelve horses, greyhounds and their accoutrements, which he plans to exchange for the pigs. Math goes to war, Gwydion kills Pryderi by magic. Gilfaethwy rapes Goewin in the ensuing chaos.

When Math discovers what has happened, he marries Goewin, and Gwydion and Gilfaethwy are punished by being transformed into beasts in whose shapes they are made to couple as male and female in compensation for the rape of Goewin. The are transformed in the following shapes:

Gwydion	Gilfaethwy
stag	hind
sow	boar
wolf	bitch

and three children are born of their union.

Gwydion suggests his sister, Arianrhod, as an alternative footholder, since this position must be held by a virgin, but she births two children, Dylan and Llew, on stepping over Math's wand. Gwydion raises Llew as his own child but is unable to get Arianrhod to acknowledge the boy. Gwydion makes himself and Llew into shoemakers in order to get a name for Llew; then he turns them both into poets, and tricks Arianrhod into arming Llew. Finally he has to make a wife out of flowers, with the aid of Math:

Blodeuwedd

Not of mother, nor of father was my creation.
I was made from the ninefold elements:
From fruit-trees, from paradisal fruit;
From primroses and hillflowers,
From blossom of the trees and bushes;
From the roots of the earth I was made;
From the bloom of the nettle,
From water of the ninth wave.
Math enchanted me before I was made immortal;
Gwydion created me by his magic wand;
From Emrys and Euryon, from Mabon and Modron,
From five fifties of magicians and masters like Math was I made.
I was made by the master in his highest ecstasy;
By the wisest of druids I was made before the world began.
– Cad Goddeu (my trans.)[78]

111

After Llew's attempted assassination by Blodeuwedd's lover, Llew is transformed into eagle's shape. Gwydion finds his nephew, perched on a tree top, his decompsing flesh falling to the ground where it is eaten by a sow. With his wand, Gwydion transforms Llew back into human, if wasted, shape again, He then enchants Blodeuwedd, his creation into an owl.

In this story two generations are transformed: Gwydion and Gilfaethwy, Llew and Blodeuwedd.

THE GUARDIANS OF MEMORY

There remain those great guardians of tradition, the immortals, whose memory serves to restore the history of the ages to their successors.

Fintan, the son of Bith (which means 'Life'), is one such, who returns to Tara after having spent many ages in many shapes, in order to tell the company about the history and natural disposition of Ireland. He has lived so long that he recalls a time when an Otherworldly being came to Ireland bearing a branch of the axial tree of the Otherworld. From the berries and nuts of this branch were grown the greatest trees of Ireland. Fintan remembers these trees being felled to make barrels which have since decayed with age. His prodigious memory is passed onto the storytellers and poets of Ireland.[4]

The story of the origin of Loch Neagh gives another instance of long life. In this, Liban, the daughter of Eochaid map Mairid was the sole survivor of her family, which was drowned when the well-guardian failed to replace the cover on the magical well which overflows. She lived for a year in an underground chamber with her dog until she wished herself into the shape of a salmon, but she was transformed into a mermaid and her dog into an otter. She lived 300 years, until her singing was heard by Beoc who brought her out. She was baptised by Comgall as Muirghen or Sea-Born and was conveyed to heaven by horned deer.[54,14]

Tuan mac Carill was the sole survivor of Partholon's company. He survived endless ages in various shapes, becoming ever wiser. He became a stag, an eagle, a salmon and was eventually eaten by Cairill's wife to become a man again.[95]

These are a few of the many stories detailing those whose memories are the true guardians of traditional lore. They have lived through many ages, in many shapes and theirs is the true remembrance.

CELTIC MYTH AND MAGIC TODAY

From the depths of time to the present may seem a great leap, but unless the reader can join hands, minds and hearts with these long-lived guardians, then the Celtic tradition is surely at an end.

The past century has seen a great upsurge in interest, on many levels, in matters Celtic. Many people are interested, not only in reviving the Celtic tradition, but in making it practically applicable to their lives. What effect has this had?

At the far end of this revival, we find an overwhelming use of Celtic deities in everyday life, a tendency to reckon time from the Celtic calendrical festivals, a greater knowledge of the old stories, if only in science fantasy forms.

But is there a genuine magical tradition which we can inhabit today? Many things have been lost, not least of which is the physicality of the tradition. The practices of Native American culture, still vigorous after a hundred years or so of persecution, show the holistic way of a spirituality which is lived on every level. There are many overlaps between the Native American and Celtic traditions, which show to what extent the Celtic tradition needs animating. The traditions of spiritual quest, of shamanic vision, the purification of the sweat-lodge, the veneration of ancestral lore, are but a few common practices.

Birth in a Celtic country, ability to speak a Celtic language, do not in themselves constitute a passport to the magical and mythical worlds of the Celts. We need first the baptism of desire, to have the silver branch placed in our hands by the people of the *sidhe*, to find the secret language of poets upon our tongues, to hear the birds of Rhiannon. These are the true passports to a continuance of the Celtic tradition.

Our lives must be firmly committed to the great chain of existences if we are to partake of the beauty of the Celtic realms or to reconstitute them in our own time.

Myth and magic are generally conceived to be false and misleading doctrines in our society, things wrought of fantasy or of evil. As we have seen in this book, the primal Celtic world, like all native traditions, derives from both myth and magic its life and continuance. Myth describes the patterns and ordering of the world, while magic governs the regulation of daily life in conformity with this primal order. How we came to lose this insight is the history and cause of our present misfortunes, of our fractured and fragmented existence which is out of harmony with the natural laws. For the gods are nothing but the forces of those laws in manifest form, and the magic of the *aos dána* is their gift and means of communication between themselves and humankind.

CODA

THE SONG OF LONG LIFE

I invoke the seven daughters of the sea
Who fashion the threads of the sons of long life.
May three deaths be taken from me!
May seven waves of good fortune be dealt to me!
May no evil spirits harm me on my circuit!
In flashing corslet without hindrance!
May my fame not perish!
May old age come to me, may death not come to me till I am old!

I invoke Senach of the seven periods of time.
Whom fairy women have reared on the breasts of plenty.
May my seven candles not be extinguished!
I am an indestructible stronghold.
I am an unshaken rock.
I am a precious stone.
I am the luck of the week.
May I live a hundred times a hundred years.
Each hundred of them apart!
I summon their boons to me.
May the grace of the Holy Spirit be upon me![79]

5th century Irish
trans. by Kuno Meyer

EXERCISES

To those of us who are exiled from our native tradition by time, place or education, there are ways of sharing the inner Celtic world by simple meditative means. The simplicity of the following exercises may be deceiving to the eye, but before you pass judgement upon them, try them with your heart.

Read through each one carefully and ascertain that you are in a fit state to perform them – i.e. not drunk, depressed, angry or out of sympathy with the material. Make sure you have time and space to perform them – i.e. that you will be undisturbed by callers, children or the telephone.

Allow lots of time for each exercise. Don't be afraid to repeat it if you are dissatisfied with the results. The sharpening of concentration and application will bring improvements. Don't rush through them all in a few days, but do one at a time until you get results. If you are a person who needs discipline to perform a scheduled meditation, then be firm and stick to a predetermined but realistic pattern of practice.

BASIC CENTRING RITUAL

This exercise takes you to the Tree of Tradition. Here all wisdom and knowledge is stored. It stands at the centre of the Otherworld. Do the exercise before you attempt any of the others or when you need to be refreshed and centred.

Visualise a dolmen arch: two upright stones over which another stone has been laid. The opening is covered by a door-curtain of curious weave. See the sign which is woven on its centre and pass beyond into the Otherworld. The great tree is before you; mighty and enduring as the ages. You may see it as any long-living tree known to you. Do not be surprised to see upon its branches blossom, fruit or nuts simultaneously, for it belongs to all ages and times, all conditions and seasons. Go now and lean with your back to it, or sit at its base and feel the power coursing through the tree. Power is drawn out of the ground and circulated to the branches. Whoever sits under the tree receives and shares this circulation of power and cleansing energy. Feel your whole body as part of this network of life, tradition and energy. When you walk away through the dolmen arch, be aware of refreshment in every part of your body.

THE LORICA OF BLESSINGS

Examine some of the lorica prayers and invocations given in Chapter 9. These are personal invocations which were created for special needs. To create your own lorica, make a list of what you are most afraid of; then consider your special strengths and talents; lastly, decide which deities or saints you wish to help protect and bless you. Using all your skills and imagination, make a lorica which can be repeated at any time to yourself. You can also make a lorica of blessings and protection for other people very dear to you, or for an animal. The custom of blessing and acknowledging vulnerability by making protective invocations is one deeply ingrained in the Celtic spirit. This exercise can be adapted in many ways for modern use. Indeed, readers may wish to make a lorica for the planet earth itself.

If you wish, make a short protective lorica to be recited before you attempt any of the exercises which follow.

POET'S BED

We read about the poetic schools on p. 45. Nowhere in the modern world can we find or reconstruct such a Celtic education. However, we can place ourselves in alignment with an inner teacher of this tradition, if we so wish, and we can find a measure of natural poetic skill in our own make-up which can be trained. The problem with the following exercise is that you may fall asleep. The trick is to be at ease and lying down, but not so comfortable that you doze off. Presumably this is why Scots Gaelic poets lay with a stone on their stomachs!

Lie in a darkened room on a bed or couch. Place a blanket, scarf or shawl over your eyes or face; it should block out the light but still allow you to breathe. To stop youself dozing off, position some object under or on your body which will prevent you from being so comfortable that you lose concentration. (A hair or clothes brush under your shoulder might work!)

The purpose of this exercise is to find a poem. Lying in a darkened room will aid concentration and give sufficient stillness for you to be able to penetrate the levels which lie between you and your own creativity. Poetry is like a steady stream running undergound, only we are seldom aware of it. This exercise allows you to access that stream.

You are not attempting to make a poem on a particular theme, but be sensitive to images which arise. You may hear snatches of a poem or of music and rhythm. Do not clutch at these, but let the theme build slowly. Hold the cumulative impression in your head for as long as you can before you attempt to write anything down. Indeed, you should let it remain, in totality, for as long as possible. Celtic poets did not, of course, write things down at all, but remembered their poetic visions. We are not so skilled, although this exercise can increase one's facility. It is advisable, if you are particularly forgetful, to have a tape-recorder running, just in case!

This exercise can also be used to incubate any creative activity; the period of incubation can help the growth of any creative plans which are already seeded but not yet manifest.

The Three Inspirations

The Inspiration of the Masters is a skill which cannot be reproduced with exactitude in this century (see p. 54). The Celts lived in a time when food was so organically produced that the magical consumption of ritual or totemic meats undoubtedly had an effect. The texts do not say, but it seem obvious to the reader, that to practise *imbas forosna*, practitioners would first of all be fasting before they ate any meat. In this century, of course, many people are vegetarian and this skill has passed us by, if only by virtue of our present treatment of and production of food from animal sources.

The following exercise combines something of all three divinatory practices of *imbas forosna*, *teinm laeghda*, and *dichetal do chennaib*, since it uses incubation, psychometry and poetic invocation. Its purpose is to discover, by psychometry and poetic invocation, knowledge of certain objects, things or situations. You might, for example, wish to know more about a house you intend to buy, or a job you have applied for; in these cases you would need to hold something to do with the house or job – an estate agent's information sheet or a job application form. You might wish to discover the history and background of an object you have acquired. (Note: if you intend to practise pure psychometry on an object whose origin is unknown to you, *always* recite your lorica invocation first as a protective measure.)

In order to practise this exercise you will need to be fasting. Use your common sense and do not over-extend this period without professional advice. For most people, forgoing one meal will be a sufficient fast. Lie down, as in the 'Poet's Bed' exercise above, holding the object or information in your hand in a relaxed way. Allow the impressions to rise and, as they do so, speak them aloud in the manner of a poetic invocation. For this, you might wish to have a tape-recorder running, as in the exercise above. Always check your findings, if possible, and trust your instinctive gut-reaction over any other considerations.

FINDING YOUR PERSONAL TOTEM

This exercise enables you to find your personal totem beast by which you can transcend the ego-bound condition of humanity and align yourself with the wider creation. Your totem beast or power-animal, as it is sometimes called in shamanic circles, gives you guidance and encouragement as well as some of the deeper teachings. To know your personal totem and to work practically with it brings you to a level of healing and alignment which will centre your whole being.

Lie on your right side, breathe deeply and evenly and visualise the great tree of tradition of your basic centring exercise. This time you see the Wild Herdsman seated beneath it. He is huge, swarthy-skinned and full of primal power. On his head are horns, and in his hand a club. All the beasts of the world are in his guardianship. Approach him and ask for the knowledge of your guardian, totem beast. At this point, he may question you and set tasks or riddles; in which case, these must be undertaken before you can proceed. He may also refuse you at this time, but if you are determined and purposeful, then persist, returning another day to question him. If the Wild Herdsman, who is also known as the Guardian, accepts you and grants you knowledge, he will strike his club against the tree. In the clearing before you will appear your personal totem. Take and accept whatever beast, bird, fish or reptile you see first. It should rush towards you out of the clearing and merge with you.

If you are unsuccessful, try again. If you are still unsure or distrustful of your own judgement, your totem will make itself known in many other ways – through dreams, visions, impressions and coincidences which confirm your judgement.

If you are successful in your quest, keep in continuous relationship with your totem. Commune with it, listen to it, ask it questions. It will throw up many life challenges in the course of time.

WOOD-WISDOM

Utilising the lists in Chapter 5, practise writing inscriptions in ogham: your name or magical name, your aspirations, your personal deities and guardians are all suitable. If you can cut and inscribe a stave of wood, then the real magic of this exercise will be apparent. Take only as much wood as you need from the living tree, strip the bark and shape the stave so that it is squared off along one side. This is where you will inscribe your oghams. This stave can become talismanic, to be thrust into an earth-altar, as a reminder and token of your intent.

See if you can create your own ogham alphabet, using different criteria: god-names, plants, totem-animals, etc. e.g.

B	Boann	borage	badger
L	Lugh	lungwort	lapwing
F	Fintan	foxglove	falcon
S	Scathach	speedwell	seal
N	Nuadu	nightshade	newt, etc.

If your list of criteria also correspond, you will have a new application for your Celtic studies.

THE AUGURY OF BRIGIT

The augury of Brigit and Mary is possibly part of a lost Celtic technique which has miraculously been preserved within Christianity. The story runs that when Christ was lost in the temple, both Mary and Brigit, his foster-mother, made this augury in order to find him again.

> The augury Brigit made for her Foster-son,
> She made a pipe within her palms:
> 'I see the Foster-son by the well's side,
> Teaching the people assuredly.[35]

The augury or *frist* was made following certain conditions: the augurer was fasting, with bare head and feet. The augury was to be performed on Monday morning, before sunrise, and the augurer had to pray and meditate upon the matter. He or she recited a verse, such as the one above, while walking three times deosil around the household fire. For the purposes of this exercise, these conditions should be practically modified by the practitioner.

This exercise can be used to find lost things or to envisage things far distant. Two methods can be used: (a) sit in a quiet place, in a dim light. With fingertips and thumbs touching, make a circle of your hands and gaze, without undue strain, into the dark centre. Take your first impressions as correct, whether you 'see' with your physical or mental vision; (b) Stand in the doorway of your house and clasp with each hand the jambs of the door. Standing on the threshold with closed eyes for a few moments, see what objects, people or animals appear and make your augury according to what you see. This last exercise is a much more complex way of skrying, demanding much discipline and at least some preparation.

FINDING YOUR DESTINY

In the Celtic hero cycles, characters often have a destiny sworn upon them at their birth, but while each of us has a destiny to fulfil, becoming aware of it is not always easy. We often train for a particular job or profession while adolescent and later find ourselves drawn to something else very strongly. This exercise is for people of all ages, for it is never too late to recognise and act upon your destiny.

Go throught the dolmen door and emerge into an open courtyard in which a fountain bubbles up. Recognise this place as one of the houses of the *sidhe*. The queen of this house appears and bids you drink from the fountain of vision, so that your inner faculties become clear. She then gives you three gifts or true inner visions. She will give you your real, inner name. This name represents your true identity in the Otherworld and is a source of great power to you. She also gives you an implement, emblematic of your true destiny. (For instance, a sword, a distaff, a plough or wand, etc.) Lastly, she bids you look into the waters of the fountain where they run into a quiet pool. Look into its mirrorlike depths and clearly see yourself performing some active part of your destiny. She bids you be true to these three visions and you return through the dolmen arch.

MAKING AN EARTH SHRINE

This exercise is a way of earthing your Celtic researches in truth. Making shrines is a very Celtic activity. At almost every spring or tree, small tokens of acknowledgement were to be found in honour of the genius of the place. In our frequently profaned world, the making of shrines is a laudable activity, reaffirming that the created world is holy and that it is in continual communion with the Otherworld.

If you are lucky enough to have a garden, mark out a small area for your shrine, creating what earth shapes seem most appropriate to you. Return to your childhood sandpit in imagination and really enjoy making a miniature landscape, using stones or pieces of wood to create the shape. Next, plant bulbs, flowers or little saplings so that they will grow in your landscape. You may wish to place specific symbols or god-forms in your landscape – images you have made yourself from natural materials. You can make a cave of stones to house such an image.

If you have no garden, get the largest pot or tank of earth you can readily house and make a landscape in miniature. You may only have room for one plant or bulb in your pot, but this doesn't matter, as long as it houses growing things. Your earth-shrine will then need to be consecrated by a short ritual of your devising. You may wish to dedicate it to a specific god or saint, to walk deosil around it, to bless the earth and the other elements within your shrine.

However you proceed, remember that to create a shrine is to be responsible for it. It will need your attention and care if it is to remain sacred. The year's turning will modify your shrine. You will need to weed it, replant it, reshape it.

This exercise can have wider applications. All around us lie untended wastelands where rubbish accumulates and vandalism is rife. With your friends and neighbours, adopt such a site and attempt to clean it up, with your local council's help if necessary. Some pieces of ground frequently turn out to be council property and can often be turned over to the use of neighbourhood schemes, playgrounds, etc. You can consecrate such sites to helpful deities such as the Dagda or Anu, who are deeply concerned with the protection of the land, and ask them to help you. The guardianship of your native earth starts in your own locality. By taking care of one small part of it, you extend the area of your personal earth-shrine a hundredfold.

BIBLIOGRAPHY

All books are published in London, unless otherwise stated.

TEXTUAL SOURCES

1. Adamnan *Life of St Columba*, trans. J. T. Fowler, Oxford, Clarendon Press, 1894
2. Allchin, A. M., and De Waal, Esther (eds.), *Threshold of Light: Prayers and Praises from the Celtic Tradition*, Darton, Longman & Todd, 1986
3. Best, R. I., 'The Adventures of Art, Son of Conn, and the Courtship of Delbchaem', in *Eriu* 3, pp. 149–73, 1906
4. Best, R. I. *The Settling of the Manor of Tara*, in *Eriu* 4, part 2, pp. 121 *et seq.*, 1910
5. Calder, G. *Auraicept na N'Eces* (The Scholar's Primer) Edinburgh, John Grant, 1917
6. Cross, T. P., and Slover, C. H. *Ancient Irish Tales*, Dublin, Figgis, 1936
7. Dillon, Miles, *Cycles of the Irish Kings*, Geoffrey Cumberledge/Oxford University Press, 1946
8. Gantz, Jeffrey, *Early Irish Myths and Sagas*, Harmondsworth, Penguin, 1981
9. Geoffrey of Monmouth, *History of the Kings of Britain*, Harmondsworth, Penguin, 1966
10. Geoffrey of Monmouth *Vita Merlini*, trans. J. J. Parry, Illinois, University of Illinois Press, 1925

11. Gerald of Wales, *The History and Topography of Ireland*, trans. John O'Meara, Harmondsworth, Penguin, 1982

12. Gerald of Wales, *The Journey Through Wales*, trans. Lewis Thorpe, Harmondsworth, Penguin, 1978

13. Jackson, Kenneth Hurstone, *A Celtic Miscellany*, Routledge & Kegan Paul, 1951

14. Joyce, P. W., *Old Celtic Romances*, C. Kegan Paul, 1879

15. *Lenor Gabála Erenn* (The Book of the Taking of Ireland) (5 vols.), trans. R. A. Stewart Macalister, Dublin, Irish Texts Soc., 1938, 1939, 1940, 1941, 1956

16. 'Life of St Brigit', in *Lives of the Saints*, trans. W. Stokes, Oxford, 1890 (Anecdota Oxoniensia, Medieval & Modern Series, No. 5)

17. *The Mabinogion*, trans. Lady Charlotte Guest, Ballantyne Press, 1910

18. *The Metrical Dindsenchas* (5 parts), trans. Edward Gwynn, Dublin, Hodges, Figgis & Co., 1903–1935

19. Meyer, Kuno, *Ancient Irish Poetry*, Constable, 1913–

20. Meyer, Kuno, *Death Tales of the Ulster Heroes*, in *Royal Irish Academy Todd Lecture Series*, vol. XIV, Dublin, Hodges, 1906

21. Meyer, Kuno, *The Voyage of Bran, Son of Febal*, David Nutt, 1895

22. Nennius, *British History and the Welsh Annals*, Phillimore & Co., 1980

23. Pliny, *Natural History VI*, trans. W. H. S. Jones, Heinemann, 1951

24. 'The Prose Tales in the Rennes Dindsenchas', ed. and trans. Whitley Stokes, in *Revue Celtique* 15, pp. 272–336, 418–84; 16, pp. 31–83, 135–67, 269–312

25. *Sanas Chormaic* (*Cormac's Glossary*) trans. John O'Donovan, ed. Whitley Stokes, Calcutta, O. T. Cutter, 1868

26. Scarre, A. M. 'The Beheading of John the Baptist by Mog Ruith', in *Eriu* 4, pp. 170–81, 1910

27. *Senchus Mor* (Ancient Laws of Ireland), (5 vols.) Dublin, Alexander Thom, 1865

28. Stokes, Whitley, trans., 'The Colloquy of the Two Sages', *Revue Celtique* 26, 1905, pp. 4–64

29. Stokes, Whitley, trans., 'The Calendar of Oengus', in *Transactions of the Royal Irish Academy* vol. I, Dublin, Hodges, Foster & Figgis, 1880

30. *Tain Bo Cuailnge* (The Cattle Raid of Cooley) trans. Thomas

Kinsella, Dublin, Dolmen Press, 1970

31. *Trioedd Ynys Prydein* (The Welsh Triads) ed. and trans. Rachel Bromwich, Cardiff, Univ. of Wales Press, 1961

32. Ua Nuallain, Tómas P., trans. *A Prayer to the Archangels for Each Day of the Week*, MS 23. P. 3, R.I.A., Fo. 19. (Irish MS in the Bodleian Library)

33. Warren, F. E. *The Liturgy and Ritual of the Celtic Church* Woodbridge, Boydell Press, 1987

THE CELTS IN FOLK TRADITION

34. Campbell, J. F., *Popular Tales of the West Highlands* (4 vols.), Wildwood Press, 1983–4

35. *Carmina Gadelica* (6 vols.) trans. Alexander Carmichael, Edinburgh, Scottish Academic Press, 1972

36. Curtin, Jeremiah, *Hero Tales of Ireland*, Macmillan, 1894

37. Mackenzie, Donald A., *Wonder Tales from Scottish Myth and Legend*, Glasgow, Blackie & Son, 1917

38. Wimberley, Lowry Charles, *Folklore in the English and Scottish Ballads*, Chicago, Univ. of Chicago Press, 1928

39. Young, Ella, *Celtic Wonder Tales*, Edinburgh, Floris Books, 1985

GENERAL BOOKS

40. Bamford, Christopher, and Marsh, William Price, *Celtic Christianity*, Edinburgh, Floris Books, 1986

41. Byrne, F. J., *Irish Kings and High Kings*, Batsford, 1973

42. Carney, James, and Greene, David, eds., *Celtic Studies*, Routledge & Kegan Paul, 1968

43. Corkery, Daniel, *The Hidden Ireland*, Dublin, Gill & Macmillan, 1967

44. Cunliffe, Barry *The Celtic World*, Bodley Head, 1979

45. De Jubainville, H. Arbois, *The Irish Mythological Cycle*, trans. Richard Irvine, Dublin, O'Donoghue and Co, 1903

46. Delaney, Frank, *A Walk in the Dark Ages*, Collins, 1988

47. Dillon, Myles, and Chadwick, Nora, *The Celtic Realms*, New York, New American Library, 1967

48. Dillon, Myles, *The Taboos of the Kings of Ireland* (no details)

49. Dinneen, Patrick S., *Irish-English Dictionary*, Dublin, Irish Texts Society, 1927

50. Farmer, David Hugh, *The Oxford Dictionary of Saints*, Oxford, Clarendon Press, 1978
51. Finlay, Ian, *Columba*, Gollancz, 1979
52. *Gairdín an Anama: Leabhar Urnaithe an Phobail*, Dublin, Am Sagart, Má Nuad, 1977
53. Graves, Robert, *The White Goddess*, Faber, 1961
54. Gregory, Lady, *The Voyage of St Brendan the Navigator and Stories of the Saints of Ireland*, Gerrard's Cross, Colin Smythe, 1973
55. Guyonvarc'h, Christian-J., *Textes Mythologiques Irlandais I*, Rennes, Ogam-Celticum, 1980
56. Guyot, Charles, *The Legend of the City of Ys*, Amherst, Univ. of Massachusetts Press, 1979
57. Hanna, W. A., *Celtic Migrations*, Belfast, Pretani Press, 1985
58. Henderson, George, *Survivals in Belief among the Celts*, Glasgow, James Maclehose, 1911
59. Herm, Gerhard, *The Celts*, Weidenfeld & Nicolson, 1976
60. Humphries, Emyr, *The Taliesin Tradition*, Black Raven Press, 1983
61. Joyce, P. W., *A Social History of Ancient Ireland*, Longmans, Green & Co., 1903
62. Keating, Geoffrey, *The History of Ireland* (4 vols.), Irish Texts Soc., 1902, 1908, 1914
63. Le Roux, Françoise, 'Le Dieu Druide et le Druide Divin', *Ogam* 12, 1960, pp. 349–82.
64. Le Roux, Françoise, and Guyonvarc'h, Christian-J., *Les Druides* Rennes, Ouest-France, 1986
65. Le Roux, Françoise, and Guyonvarc'h, Christian-J., *Mórrígan – Bodh – Macha; La Souveraineté Guerriére de L'Irlande*, Rennes, Ogam–Celticum, 1983
66. Löffer, Christa Maria, *The Voyage to the Otherworld Island in Early Irish Literature* (Doctoral dissertation in 2 parts) Salzburg, Institute Für Anglistik und Amerikanistik, Universität Salzburg, 1983
67. Mac Cana, Proinsias *The Learned Tales of Medieval Ireland*, Dublin, Dublin Institute for Advanced Studies, 1980
68. Macleod, Fiona (William Sharp), *The Winged Destiny*, New York, Lemma Pub. Corp. 1974
69. Macneill, John T., *The Celtic Churches: a History* AD 200–1200 Chicago, Univ. of Chicago Press, 1974
70. Maher, Michael, ed., *Irish Spirituality*, Dublin, Veritas Publications, 1981

71. Markale, Jean, *Celtic Civilization*, Gordon Cremonesi, 1978
72. Matthews, Caitlín, *Arthur and the Sovereignty of Britain*, Arkana, 1989
73. Matthews, Caitlín, *Mabon and the Mysteries of Britain*, Arkana, 1987
74. Matthews, Caitlín and John, *The Western Way* (2 vols.) Arkana, 1985, 1986
75. Matthews, John, *The Elements of the Arthurian Legend*, Shaftesbury, Element Books, 1989
76. Matthews, John, *The Elements of the Grail Tradition*, Shaftesbury, Element Books, 1990
77. Matthews, John, *Gawain, Knight of the Goddess*, Aquarian Press, Wellingborough, 1990
78. Matthews, John and Caitlín, *Taliesin: the Shamanic Mysteries of Britain*, Unwin Hyman 1990
79. Meyer, Kuno, *Learning in Ireland in the Fifth Century and the Transmission of Letters*, Dublin, School of Irish Learning, 1913
80. Monard, J., *A Druidic Calendar: The Coligny Calendar As Cleared Up*, privately printed.
81. Montague, John, ed., *The Faber Book of Irish Verse*, Faber, 1974
82. Naddair, Kaledon, *Keltic Folk and Faerie Tales*, Century, 1987
83. Naddair, Kaledon, *Ogham, Koelbren and Runic: Shamanistic Divination Scripts of Britain and Europe*, Edinburgh, Inner Keltia Publications, 1986
84. North, F. J., *Sunken Cities*, Cardiff, Univ. of Wales Press, 1957
85. Nyberg, T., ed., *History and Heroic Tale: A Symposium*, Odense Univ. Press, 1985
86. O'Boyle, Sean, *Ogam – the Poet's Secret*, Dublin, Gilbert Dalton, 1980
87. O'Cathasaigh, Tomás, *The Heroic Biography of Cormac mac Airt*, Dublin, Dublin Institute for Advanced Studies, 1977
88. O'Currey, Eugene, *On the Manners and Customs of the Ancient Irish*, Williams & Norgate, 1873
89. O'Dwyer, Peter O. C., *Céli Dé*, Dublin, Editions Tailliura, 1977
90. O'hogain, Daithi *Fionn Mac Cumhail* Dublin, Gill & Macmillan, 1988

91. O'hogain, Daithi, *The Hero in Irish Folk History*, Dublin, Gill & Macmillan, 1986
92. Ó'Súilleabháin, Séan, 'Etiological Stories in Ireland', in *Medieval Literature and Folklore Studies Presented to F. Uttley* (no other details)
93. *Oxford Dictionary of the Christian Church*, ed. F. L. Cross, Oxford, Oxford Univ. Press, 1958
94. Quinn, Bob, *Atlantean: Ireland's North African and Maritime Heritage*, Quartet, 1986
95. Rees, Alwyn and Brinley, *Celtic Heritage*, Thames & Hudson, 1961
96. Renfrew, Colin, *Archaeology and Language: The Puzzle of Indo-European Origins*, Cape, 1987
97. Ross, Anne, *Pagan Celtic Britain*, Routledge & Kegan Paul, 1967
98. Sjoestedt, Marie-Louise, *Gods and Heroes of the Celts*, Berkeley, Turtle Island Foundation, 1982
99. Stover, Leon E. and Kraig, Brian, *Stonehenge: The Indo-European Tradition*, Chicago, Nelson-Hall, 1978
100. Sutherland, Elizabeth, *Ravens and Black Rain*, Constable, 1983
101. Wagner, H., *The Origins of Pagan Celtic Religion*, Zeitschrift fur Celtische Philologie XXXVIII, 1981 pp. 1–28
102. Wagner, H. 'Studies in the Origin of Early Celtic Tradition', Eriu 26, 1975, pp. 1–26
103. Williams, Gwyn A. *When Was Wales?*, Harmondsworth, Penguin, 1985
104. Wyatt, Isabel, 'Goddess into Saint: The Foster Mother of Christ', in *The Golden Blade* pp. 55–66, 1963

DISCOGRAPHY

The following records and tapes are recommended as giving an authentic sound of the Celtic world.

THE CELTIC TRIBE

Aberjaber, *Cerddoriaeth o'r Gweledydd Celtaidd*, Sain-Cambrian 1340M
Davey, Sean, *The Pilgrim*, TARA 3011

Williamson, Robin, *Music for the Mabinogion*, Ceirnini Cladaigh CCF10

THE OTHERWORLD

Davey, Sean, *The Brendan Voyage*, Tara 3006

Matthews, Caitlín and John, *Walking the Western Way*, Sulis Music and Tapes, BCM Box 3721, London WC1N 3XX. (meditation tape)

Stewart, Bob, *The Unique Sound of the Psaltery*, Sulis Music and Tapes, BCM Box 3721, London WC1N 3XX.

Stivell, Alan, *Légende*, AZ/475

THE CELTIC CHURCH

Ní Riain, Nóirín and the Monks of Glenstal, *Caoineadh na Maighdine*, Gael-Linn CEF084

Ní Riain, Nóirín and the Monks of Glenstal, *Good People All*, Glenstal GR01

Reznikoff, Iegor, *Alleluias et Offertoires des Gaules*, Harmonia Mundi HM 40.1044

JOURNALS

Cambridge Medieval Celtic Studies, Dept of Anglo-Saxon, Norse and Celtic, 9 West Road, Cambridge CB3 9DP (2 issues a year)

This is one of the most accessible of the scholarly journals where recent Celtic scholarship is aired.

USEFUL ADDRESSES

When writing to any of these addresses, please remember an SAE or international reply-paid coupons for a response.

Keltia Publications, P.O. Box 307, Edinburgh EH9 1XA. Kaledon Naddair publishes numerous books and magazines in the Celtic and Pictish spirit, as well as selling other artefacts. He also runs a College of Druidism.

Order of Bards, Ovates and Druids, 260 Kew Road, Richmond, Surrey TW9 3EG – the Order runs a correspondence course and numerous other activities in the spirit of the Celtic

Mysteries, combining concern for the planet earth. It also runs a tree-planting programme.

Sulis Music and Tapes, BCM 3721, London WC1N 6XX issues many musical, magical and meditation tapes of Celtic interest.

Robin Williamson Productions, P.O. Box 27522, Los Angeles, Calif. 90027, USA issue many tapes of Celtic storytelling and song, arranged and performed by a modern bard.

INDEX